To John Bunnel,

And our shared quest.

R.J. Lifton

Feb. 1971

Books by Robert Jay Lifton

Death in Life: Survivors of Hiroshima

Thought Reform and the Psychology of Totalism: A Study
    of "Brainwashing" in China

Revolutionary Immortality

History and Human Survival

Birds

BOUNDARIES

BY ROBERT JAY LIFTON

BOUNDARIES

PSYCHOLOGICAL MAN IN REVOLUTION

 RANDOM HOUSE   NEW YORK

Library of Congress Catalog Card Number: 70-117686
Acknowledgments   Chapter 1: reprinted by permission
from *Death in Life*, Random House, 1967. Chapter 3:
reprinted by permission from *Revolutionary
Immortality*, Random House, 1968. Chapter 4: from
"Protean Man," first published in the *Partisan Review*.
Chapter 5: from "The Young and the Old—Notes on
a New History," first published in the *Atlantic Monthly*.
Manufactured in the United States of America by
The Colonial Press Inc., Clinton, Mass.

9   8   7   6   5   4   3   2

First American Edition

This book contains five half-hour talks
first broadcast during January of
1969 in *Ideas*, a radio series of the
CBC Information Programs Department.

FOR KENNETH JAY LIFTON—
NEW BOUNDARIES

INTRODUCTION

People everywhere find it increasingly difficult to give significant form to their ideas, their tools, themselves. Our legacy of holocausts and dislocations have left us confused about limits, no longer certain about where anything begins or ends. Hence, the theme of "Life Boundaries," suggested by the Canadian Broadcasting Corporation for a series of radio talks, struck me as one highly appropriate to our psychological and historical predicament. It also had direct bearing upon my own investigative struggles with some of the most destructive, and potentially revitalizing, forces of contemporary 'psychohistory.'

One response to the crisis of boundaries is a desperate attempt to hold fast to all existing categories, to keep all definitions pure. This is, unfortunately, the impulse of a great deal of political, military, and cultural thought throughout the world, including that of classical Marxism and classical psychoanalysis. More than being merely conservative, this response is a *reaction* to a perceived threat of chaos; it all too readily lends itself to nostalgic visions of restoring a golden age of exact boundaries, an age in which men allegedly knew exactly where they stood. The approach is self-defeating and, moreover, impossible to maintain.

The opposite response is to destroy, or seek to destroy, all boundaries, in the name of an all-encompassing oneness. Norman O. Brown, for instance, holds up the model of Dionysus, "the mad god [who] breaks down the boundaries; releases the prisoners; abolishes repression; and abolishes the *principium individuationist,* substituting for it the unity of man and the unity of man with nature." Quite simply, according to Brown, "The conclusion of the whole matter is, break down the boundaries, the walls." But this impulse to eliminate all boundaries confuses a great mythological vision (embodying a basic component of the imagination) with a 'solution' for man's problems of living. The approach all too readily collapses into a pseudo-instinctualism in which the only heroes are the infant, the pre-human animal, and the schizophrenic.

Though seemingly antagonistic to one another, these two absolute responses share a schematic disdain for history, and for man's symbol-forming connection with history. Were they our only approaches to the question of boundaries, they would, if anything, escalate our present spiritual warfare with ourselves, and at the same time render it more static.

There is, however, an alternative. Boundaries can be viewed as neither permanent nor by definition false, but rather as essential and yet subject to the fundamental forces for change characterizing our age. We require images of limit and restraint, if only to help us grasp what we are transcending. We need distinctions between our biology and our history, all the more so as we seek to bring these together in a sense of ourselves that is unprecedentedly fluid and tenuous. In speaking of boundaries of destruction, of death and life, of the self, or revolution, and of the New History, I bring together various strands of my work, each discussed in greater detail elsewhere but now woven around, and specifically addressed to, one overall issue: the breakdown and re-creation of the boundaries of our existence. I end up with no definitive conclusions, no permanent 'walls,' but only with a series of specters, directions, and possibilities.—*R. J. L.*

CONTENTS

DESTRUCTION

This is a time to talk about boundaries. I say this not only because man has so recently completed his first trip to the area of the moon, and what may really be more important from a psychological standpoint, achieved his first escape from, or perhaps transcendence of, the gravitational field of the earth—in a sense his first escape from the authority of the earth. That would of course be reason enough. But long before that flight, man's history—one could say his entire modern history—has been characterized by a series of breakdowns and blurrings of boundaries. And since World War II that process has become so intense and so extreme that we may take the year 1945 as the beginning of a new historical epoch.

The atomic bombings of Hiroshima and Nagasaki were by no means the only significant, or tragic, events of that year, but they did have overwhelming importance for the subject I wish to discuss first: the boundaries of destruction.

I base my discussion on six months of research I conducted in Hiroshima in 1962, mostly through interviews with survivors of the first atomic bomb, and upon my efforts ever since to look further into the importance of that event. I chose the title *Death in Life* for the book in which I described my Hiroshima work because I felt that that particular phrase, more than any other, epitomized the entire atomic bomb experience of the city, in ways I shall in a moment try to make clear. Yet there are many forms of death in life which have little to do with Hiroshima, so the question arises: What was special about the kind of death in life produced by the atomic bomb? The answer, or at least one answer, lies in the realm of boundaries of destruction. I shall speak of the breakdown of these boundaries, not so much in the material as in the psychological sense; that is, in relationship to altered images and symbols. Since we as human beings think and act, really live, on the basis of such images and symbols, I will really be discussing, in this chapter as in the others, changes in the boundaries of existence.

Now in the case of ordinary weapons—an arrow shot from a bow, a bullet from a gun, or a bomb dropped from a plane—people are killed or injured, the community around them suffers its losses and dislocations, and although there are inevitably long-range repercussions, there is also a clear sense of limits. One buries the dead, nurses the wounded, and reconstitutes the community with some feeling that the assault is over. Men have suffered and died, others have recovered, and that is that.

Not so with the atomic bomb. The people who happened to be in Hiroshima at eight-fifteen A.M. on August 6, 1945, experienced, from the moment of the bomb's fall, what is best described as a permanent encounter with death. We may understand this encounter as consisting of four stages.

The first was the overwhelming immersion in death directly following the bomb's fall, beginning with the terrible array of dead and near-dead in the midst of which each survivor found himself. We can begin to understand the blurring of boundaries of destruction in relationship to this first stage alone, especially when we look at the question of fatalities from the bomb. The number killed is variously estimated from sixty-three thousand to two hundred and forty thousand, or more. The official figures are usually given as seventy-eight thousand, but the city of Hiroshima estimates two hundred thousand, the total encompassing between twenty-five and fifty percent of the city's then daytime population, also a disputed figure. The enormous disparity in these estimates is related to the extreme confusion which then existed, to differing methods of calculation, and also to underlying emotional influences, quite apart from mathematical considerations, which have at times affected estimators. For all of these reasons, a really accurate estimate may never be possible.

In other words, concerning the central issue of any disaster, its destruction of human life, one cannot really say just how far this one extended. One can say that all of Hiroshima immediately became involved in it. That is, anyone exposed relatively near the center of the city could not escape from a sense of ubiquitous death around him, resulting from blast, radiant heat, and ionizing radiation, so much so that I have characterized, as the most significant psychological feature of this early stage, the sense of a sudden and absolute shift from normal existence to an overwhelming encounter with death.

Many survivors recall, as the very first emotions they experienced, feelings related to death and dying, such as: "I felt as if I was going to suffocate and then die without knowing exactly what had happened to me"; or, "My first feeling was: 'I think I will die' "; or, "This is the end for me"; or, "I was dying without seeing my parents." Now, such feelings can hardly be surprising in relationship to any disaster, but in Hiroshima this early imagery included something more: the sense that the whole world was dying.

For instance, a science professor, covered by falling debris, and temporarily blinded, put it this way: "My body seemed all black. Everything seemed dark, dark all over. Then I thought, 'the world is ending.' " A Protestant minister, responding to the scenes of mutilation and destruction he saw everywhere, after walking all through the city, told me: "The feeling I had was that everyone was dead. The whole city was destroyed. . . . I thought all of my family must be dead. It doesn't matter if I die. . . . I thought this was the end of Hiroshima, of Japan, of humankind." And a woman writer: "I just could not understand why our surroundings changed so greatly in one instant. . . . I thought it must have been something which had nothing to do with the war, the collapse of the earth, which was said to take place at the end of the world, which I had read about as a child. . . . There was a fearful silence, which made me feel that all people and all trees and all vegetation were dead."

Hiroshima victims could be said to have experienced a genuine confusion between the state of death and that of life. Later, when referring to themselves and others around them, they used such terms as "walking ghosts," "people who walked in the realm of dreams," or as one man described his sense of himself: "I was not really alive." It was in relationship to this ultimate form of existential confusion that the survivors' inner image of death in life impressed itself upon me. And the image maintained itself within survivors from then on.

The second stage of the permanent encounter with death took the form of invisible contamination. Here I refer to the unprecedented feature of nuclear weapons: the bodily effects of irradiation. For immediately after the bomb fell, sometimes within hours or even minutes, often during the first twenty-four hours or during the following days and weeks, survivors began to notice in themselves and others a strange form of illness. It consisted of fever and weakness, severe gastrointestinal symptoms, and then later, inflammation and ulceration in parts of the mouth and gums, generalized loss of scalp and bodily hair, purple spots on various parts of the body from bleeding into the skin, severe hemorrhaging from all of the body orifices, and very low white blood cell counts when these could be taken. The condition in many cases followed a progressive course until death.

These early symptoms of irradiation, which spread terror among physicians no less than ordinary people, aroused in the minds of the people of Hiroshima an image of a weapon which not only kills and destroys on a colossal scale, but also leaves behind in the bodies of those exposed to it deadly influences which may emerge at any time and strike down their victims.

The relationship of this second stage to the breakdown of boundaries is revealed most clearly, I believe, in a series of rumors which swept Hiroshima during the period immediately following the bomb.

One rumor, among the many that survivors recalled, simply held that all those who had been exposed to the bomb in Hiroshima would be dead within three years. The symbolic message here was: none can escape the poison; the epidemic is total; all shall die. But there was a second rumor, even more frequently reported to me, and, I thought, with much greater emotion: the belief that trees, grass, and flowers would never again grow in Hiroshima; from that day on the city would be unable to sustain vegetation of any

kind. The meaning here was that nature was drying up alto-
gether; life was being extinguished at its source—an ultimate form of desolation that not only encompassed human
death but went beyond it. And a third rumor, closely related to the other two, held that for a period of seventy to
seventy-five years, Hiroshima would be uninhabitable; no
one would be able to live there. Here was a sense that Hiroshima was to become totally de-urbanized, literally de-
vitalized, that the bomb's invisible contamination created something close to a permanently uninhabitable area.

Other rumors, especially during those early days, carried
these feelings even further. There were rumors that there
would be new attacks with "poison gases" or "burning oil";
that America, having dropped such a terrible "hot bomb,"
as the survivors called it, would next drop a "cold bomb" or
an "ice bomb" which would simply "freeze everything," so
that "everyone would die"; and even a rumor that America
would drop rotten pigs, so that as one man put it, "everything on the earth would decay and go bad." These addi-
tional rumors, some of them absurd in retrospect but undoubtedly terrifying at the time, conveyed the sense that the
environment had been so fundamentally disturbed, and in
such an unbelievably deadly manner, that only further and
more total deterioration and decomposition could be ex-
pected.

These rumors were inevitably associated with various
kinds of supernatural imagery, including that of the atomic
bomb as a form of cosmic retribution, a curse with which
one or one's group was afflicted for some form of wrong-
doing in this or a previous existence. In general, the second
stage left people with a feeling that there were no bounda-

ries—no limits whatsoever—to the deadly force intruding upon their world.

The third encounter with death occurred with later radiation effects, not months but years after the atomic bomb itself, and is in many ways summed up by the scientifically inaccurate but emotionally significant term 'A-bomb disease.' The medical condition which frequently became the model for 'A-bomb disease' was leukemia. For there was an actual increase in incidence of that always fatal malignancy of the blood-forming organs, first noted during the late forties and early fifties. The symptoms of leukemia closely resemble those of acute radiation effects, so that, psychologically speaking, leukemia, or the threat of leukemia, became an indefinite continuation of the earlier invisible contamination of which I have spoken.

And even as the incidence of leukemia was recognized to be diminishing, that is, approaching the normal, there has been increasing evidence accumulating that the incidence of various other forms of cancer has been increasing among survivors. This is clearly true for thyroid cancer, and is possibly true for cancer of the stomach, lung, ovary, uteran cervix and other bodily areas. Now leukemia is a rare disease, so that even with the increased incidence, cases in Hiroshima and Nagasaki believed associated with the atomic bombs number only in the hundreds. But cancer is not a rare disease, and should the trend continue, as appears likely, the increase in cancer will undoubtedly revive in survivors intense expressions of death symbolism, just as these were beginning to decline. Thus on a chronic level of bodily concern, we again see evoked the feeling that the bomb can do anything, and anything it does is likely to be fatal.

I will not attempt to elaborate on the wide variety of bodily impairments which some physicians in Hiroshima believe to be caused, or partly caused, by delayed effects of irradiation. Suspected and disputed conditions include various anemias, liver and blood diseases, endocrine and skin disorders, damage to the central nervous system, premature aging, impairments in early development, and a vague but persistently reported borderline condition of general weakness and debilitation. The relationship of the bomb to all of these conditions is medically controversial. But the point is that in the minds of survivors any kind of ailment, whether it be simple fatigue, mild anemia, fulminating leukemia or ordinary cardiovascular disease—whether there is no apparent scientific relationship to radiation effects, or whether such a relationship may be indeed presumed—becomes associated with the atomic bomb and its related death imagery. And their problem is intensified by the continuous publicizing of chronic atomic bomb effects—or 'A-bomb disease'—by mass media and by survivor and peace organizations. This publicizing is often done for very important ethical purposes, to make known the effects and the consequences of these weapons, but it does, nonetheless, increase the anxiety of survivors.

The survivor, then, becomes involved in a vicious circle on the psychosomatic plane of existence. He is likely to associate even the mildest everyday discomfort with possible radiation effects, and anything he relates to radiation effects becomes in turn associated with death. Virtually all survivors find themselves constantly plagued with what we may call a 'nagging doubt' about the possibility of radiation effects. They look upon themselves as people who are particularly vulnerable, who cannot afford to take chances. The boundaries destroyed here are those between health and disease, between bodily vitality and deadly physical impairment.

Beyond this sense of impaired body image survivors carry the fear that this impairment will manifest itself in subsequent generations—a still further extension of the impact of the bomb. Genetic effects are in many ways even more controversial as a medical issue than the other physical aftereffects just mentioned. Fortunately, studies on comparative populations have so far revealed no clear increase in genetic abnormalities among children of survivors. But it is widely known that such abnormalities *can* be caused by radiation, and there is again the problem of variation in medical opinion. Another factor in survivors' psychological associations and fears has been the definite damage from radiation experienced by children exposed *in utero,* that is, when inside of their mothers' wombs at the time of the bomb. This is a phenomenon, scientifically speaking, that is unrelated to genetic effects; it is a direct effect of irradiation upon immature, rapidly-growing, and therefore highly sensitive tissue. But ordinary people often fail to make the distinction. And these early effects *in utero* were quite terrifying. They include microcephaly (distorted, small heads) as well as mental retardation.

So, at this third stage the curse I spoke of before becomes an enduring taint of death, associated not only with the entire psychosomatic organism, but with one's posterity. Survivors, therefore, have the sense of being involved in an endless chain of potentially lethal impairment, which, if it does not appear in one year or in one generation, may well manifest itself in the next. In other words, the death taint knows no generational boundaries; the victim cannot even be sure of beginning anew, of being symbolically reborn, through his sons and daughters or their sons and daughters.

The fourth stage of the permanent encounter with death is not really a stage as such, but a lifelong identification with death, dying, and with an anonymous group of 'the dead.' Survivors in Hiroshima and Nagasaki became, in their own eyes as well as those of others, a tainted group, indeed a group whose identity has been built around precisely the inner death taint I have been discussing. That identity is symbolized externally by disfigurement, that is, by keloid scars, which although possessed by only a small minority of survivors now have come to represent the stigmata of atomic bomb exposure. This taint has expressed itself in terms of people's attitudes toward atomic bomb survivors— in the discrimination against survivors in relationship to jobs and to marriage arrangements (the latter, in Japan, usually made by families and go-betweens).

Within this identity there is a further breakdown of boundaries, which has to do with what is usually an unquestioned assumption of every man: namely, that being alive, he has the right to live. For the Hiroshima survivor, and to a lesser degree the survivor of any intense death encounter, can never, inwardly, simply conclude that it was logical and right for him and not others to survive. Rather, I would suggest, he is held to an unconscious perception of organic social balance, perhaps universal in nature, which makes him feel that his survival was made possible by others' deaths: if they had not died, he would have had to, and if he had not survived, someone else would have.

I thus encountered among Hiroshima survivors a frequent sense of being 'as-if-dead,' or what I called an 'identity of the dead,' which took the following inner sequence: I almost died; I should have died; I did die or at least am not really alive; or if I am alive, it is impure of me to be so, and anything I do which affirms life is also impure and an insult to the dead, who alone are pure. An expression of this sense of themselves can be found in the life-style of many survivors, one of marked constriction and self-abnegation, based upon the feeling that any show of vitality is in some way inappropriate for them, not inwardly permissible. They retain a sense of infinite culpability, and even, ironically enough, of guilt and of responsibility for the catastrophe itself, despite being victims rather than perpetrators of that catastrophe.

Survivors thus experience a threat to the boundary between the living and the dead that man has struggled so desperately over the course of his history to establish and maintain.

Inevitably they have had great difficulty coming to terms with their experience, giving it some acceptable inner form or meaning and placing it within what we can call a 'formulation' in the deepest sense of that term. To render their experience significant, survivors looked to some form of peace symbol—to an image of a world chastened and rendered wiser by the atomic bombings—and some have participated actively in peace movements. But such peace-centered formulations have been impeded by continuing international conflict and nuclear threat, and more immediately by ideological and personal antagonisms among groups of survivors within peace organizations. Whether engendered from without, or from within Hiroshima itself, these antagonisms violated the very strict—in fact, exaggerated—ethical requirements that survivors make of themselves and of others in regard to any activity associated with the atomic bomb. Hence, most peace efforts have been viewed as impure and unsatisfactory. Similar problems arose in regard to leadership of survivor movements of all kinds, whether the leadership was religious, scientific, aristocratic, or populist in style, or of an essentially ethical or pragmatically political kind. It has been difficult for survivors to accept as authentic such leaders as arose among them. They criticize these leaders for impure behavior of one kind or another, and ultimately for insulting the dead.

Concerning medical and economic benefits, survivors on the one hand have sought these and felt themselves in need of them, but have at the same time deeply resented virtually everything about them. The pattern here is one I call 'suspicion of counterfeit nurturance.' This is a form of tainted dependency intrinsic to any kind of victimization: the victim feels himself to require special help, but is at the same time deeply antagonistic to both help and helper because they tend to confirm within him his own sense of weakness and inferiority.

Related forms of conflict arose in relationship to memorialization, over the monuments constructed and how authentic they could be, and over the yearly commemoration of the experience and the various public ceremonies that were instituted for the atomic bomb. Survivors on the one hand feel such memorialization and commemoration to be necessary, but on the other to be unsatisfactory, inadequate, and inauthentic. The problem is virtually insoluble. For with memorialization, as with questions of special benefits, survivor movements, and the peace symbol—there is no precedent for how to absorb an atomic bomb experience, for how to deal appropriately with its extraordinary ethical and psychological demands, for how an individual person or a city should behave. Standards are obscure, boundaries extremely unclear.

The same may be said of hatred, of how to feel toward America and Americans, and of the burdens of both hatred and its absence. For it is difficult to carry about hatred over more than twenty years. It has also been difficult to find adequate objects to hate. Should one hate the pilot, the president who ordered the mission (or at least did not stop it from occurring), all Americans, or simply 'America'? As a colleague of mine once put it, "You can't hate magic." Nor has hatred been absent. Feelings toward America became bound up with other complicated and highly ambivalent emotions surrounding the American occupation, with responses to American attitudes toward nuclear weapons later on, and with the extent to which a particular survivor experienced a sense of irreparable loss (as in the case of deaths of family members) or permanent suffering or immobilization (as in the case of those who, for whatever combination of psychological and physical reasons, felt themselves unable to resume an ordinary form of existence).

There is also the question of the boundaries of trust. Survivors underwent a vast breakdown of faith in the larger human matrix supporting each individual life, indeed a loss of faith or trust in the structure of existence itself. Here, as with so many atomic-bomb problems, boundaries are both narrowed—in regard to what is inwardly considered trustworthy, authentic, or permissible—and at the same time blurred to the point of near breakdown.

One can also speak of the boundaries of artistic form, as in the case of the struggles surrounding what is called A-bomb literature—which in turn parallel in many ways struggles surrounding concentration camp literature. There are vast problems faced by writers who try in some way to capture what happened in Hiroshima or in Nazi death camps: problems of authenticity, problems of self-imposed limitations of imagination, and problems of severe creative guilt. Does one have the right to reduce such a massive event, so tragic and disturbing, to the kind of symbols that any creator must use? And even if one does, can any symbolic representation be adequate to the dimensions of the event?

But it is not only the survivors of Hiroshima who have difficulty coming to terms with the atomic bomb. We ourselves, and people throughout the world, have analogous problems of formulation. When I say, therefore, that we are all survivors of Hiroshima, I mean this to be more than a dramatic metaphor. I think we are all involved in struggles to find significance and meaning in a world in which such events can occur; and, indeed, can occur again in infinitely more extreme form, and in a way that can guarantee none of the outside help which made Hiroshima's general recovery and postwar rebuilding possible.

At the end of my book on Hiroshima, I spoke of man's having invented this kind of grotesquely absurd death. I also spoke of the general paradox of the survivor in our present, and perhaps future, world: our knowledge that great discoveries in the past have been made by survivors who could confront their historical predicament and thereby contribute to the enlargement of human consciousness; and our present inability to count upon any survivor wisdom deriving from weapons that are without limit in their capacity to destroy. We cannot count upon such wisdom because we are not at all certain that there will *be* survivors of a future war, nor that if there are survivors, they will be in any kind of condition to provide wisdom.

I spoke of Hiroshima, together with Nagasaki, as a last chance, a nuclear catastrophe from which one can still learn, from which one can derive the knowledge that could contribute to holding back the even more massive extermination these events seem to foreshadow. For I believe that our best means of reestablishing meaningful boundaries, or at least learning to live with existing ones rendered unclear and uncertain, is to confront those experiences—such as Hiroshima—which have done so much to break those boundaries down. And in this way we may contribute to man's efforts to move beyond his destructiveness in the direction of his also expanding power to create.

DEATH AND LIFE

One cannot really think seriously about Hiroshima without raising questions about nuclear weapons in general, and their influence upon that ultimate boundary between death and life.

Once more, I wish to approach the problem not in terms of the specific physical destructive power of these weapons, but of our psychological—in the broadest sense, symbolic —responses to them. For man's mental processes are such that he never notes or records a fact, a thing, or an event in a totally passive way. Rather he inwardly recreates, gives inner form to, every fact, thing, or event that impresses itself upon him. This inner recreation, his bringing something to whatever he observes or feels, is what makes man a symbolizing creature, and a formative one as well. So when I speak of his symbolic and formative responses to nuclear weapons, I am really speaking of the kind of imprint these weapons make upon his mind. And with weapons whose capacity to kill is so great as to approach infinity, only the naïve and the deluded could claim that this imprint does not, in some important way, alter the general boundaries of death and life. Unfortunately, the impact of the weapons themselves can also foster precisely such naïveté and delusion in the most dangerous ways, as I shall in a moment suggest. But I want first to say something about man's general approach to the fact of his own death, and about a theory of symbolic immortality I have attempted to develop. For I would claim that man requires a *sense* of immortality in the face of inevitable biological death. This sense of immortality need not be merely a denial of the fact of his death, though man is certainly prone to such a denial. It also represents a compelling, universal urge to maintain an inner sense of continuity, over time and space, with the various elements of life. This sense of immortality is man's way of experiencing his connection with all of human history. We can speak of it in relationship to five general modes.

First, the biological mode of immortality, the sense of living on through, but in an emotional sense, *with* or even *in* one's sons and daughters and their sons and daughters, by imagining an endless chain of biological attachment. This mode has found its classical expression in East Asian culture, especially in the traditional Chinese family system, but is of enormous importance in all cultures, and may well be the most universally significant of man's modes of immortality. Nor does it ever remain purely biological, but in varying degrees extends itself into social dimensions, into the sense of surviving through one's tribe, organization, people, nation or even species, that is, living on in any or all of these.

The second mode is the theological, as expressed both in ideas put forth by various religions concerning a life after death, and in the more general theological principle of the spiritual conquest of death. One finds expressions of the theological mode in the concepts developed by religions and cultures to suggest the acquisition of a more-than-natural power over death—in the Christian principle of grace, the Japanese idea of *kami,* and the Roman concept of numen.

A third mode is that achieved through man's works, whether through specific creative products or broader human impact, through writings, art, thought, institutions, inventions, or lasting influences of any kind upon other human beings. Thus artists, scientists, revolutionaries, social benefactors, and humble purveyors of kindness can all share in a sense of being outlived by what they have done or created.

The fourth mode is that achieved by being survived by nature itself, the sense one will live on in natural elements, limitless in space and time. One finds vivid expressions of this mode in Japanese feelings about nature, partly originating in the animism of Shinto tradition, but also in various expressions of the European Romantic movement, including the American cult of the 'great outdoors.'

A fifth mode of immortality, somewhat different from the others, depends entirely upon a psychic state—one so intense that time and death disappear. It may therefore be termed the mode of experiential transcendence, and includes various forms of ecstasy and rapture associated both with the Dionysian principle of excess, and with the mystical sense of oneness with the universe that Freud referred to as the "oceanic feeling."

What I am suggesting, then, is that the symbolic modes of immortality are not merely problems one ponders when dying. They are constantly perceived inner standards, though often indirect and outside of awareness, by which we evaluate our lives, by which we maintain feelings of connection, significance, and movement so necessary to everyday psychological existence. And if we return our attention to nuclear weapons, we can now begin to see the threats they pose to our psychological life quite independently of their use. Their very existence in the world is enough.

For, if we anticipate the possibility of nuclear weapons being used, and I believe everyone from about the age of six or seven in some measure does, we are faced with the prospect of being severed from virtually all of our symbolic paths to immortality. Thus in the post-nuclear world (if we can call it that) we can imagine no biological posterity. Without entering into the debate as to whether a general nuclear war would eliminate *all* human life on earth, or only a considerable segment of it, such is our imagery of total biological destruction that we can no longer count upon living on through (or in) family, nation, or even species. It is even quite possible that some of our present fascination with outer space, the moon, and the planets has to do with our present doubts about biological immortality on earth and with the consequent urge to discover the existence of new life, or the means of revitalizing an old life, elsewhere.

Theological immortality is also threatened. The entire modern secular historical experience had thrown it into great confusion, of course, prior to the existence of nuclear weapons. But these weapons have, for many reasons, intensified the theological crisis. In Hiroshima, for instance, people were unable to find an adequate explanation or formulation for their atomic bomb experience in the Buddhism, Shintoism, or in some cases Christianity, they had known. Nor, for the most part, even in the new religions which blossomed all through Japan after the war, and which many of the Hiroshima people embraced. None of these various forms of religious symbolism seemed adequate to the magnitude of the disaster itself.

As for the rest of us and our nuclear weapons, it is quite possible that belief in a spiritual existence beyond death cannot be effectively maintained in association with an imagined world in which there are none, or virtually none, among the biologically living. That is, one may require an assurance of the continuation of ordinary natural life, in order to be able to believe in a supernatural kind. On the other hand the weapons bring a particular insistence, even desperation, to forms of religious practice sometimes referred to as demythologizing or 'death-of-God theology,' especially where these direct themselves to immediate social and ethical issues, including those of war and peace and nuclear weapons.

Immortality through man's works, the third mode, becomes even more dubious. Following nuclear apocalypse, who can be certain of the survival of creative products, or individual kindnesses? And I think that the threat to man's works contributes to various forms of revolutionary impulse: the attempt on the part of the young both to renew these works and to alter the world in which they are so threatened, and the attempt of the old to preserve and purify what they have created—as, for instance, Mao Tse-tung's quest for revolutionary immortality which I shall discuss in a later chapter.

Nature, the fourth mode, is much more difficult to destroy, and the revived interest in man's natural environment may be more than merely an overdue reaction to our long-standing tendency to abuse it. It may, in fact, be a form of clinging to those natural forces which preceded man, and which he has always counted upon to outlast him. We might, in fact, anticipate various forms of natural theologies as a consequence of the nuclear age. But given the power of nuclear weapons, and other weapons too including biological ones, even nature is threatened.

In discussing Hiroshima, I mentioned the force of one rumor which spread throughout the city immediately after the bomb fell—the belief that trees, flowers, and grass would never again grow there—as an expression of an ultimate form of desolation which not only encompassed human death but went beyond it. Such is the power of imagery concerning the destruction of nature, and of its being lost to man.

This leaves only the fifth mode, that of experiential transcendence, which we may now see to take on a new significance. For with all the other modes so threatened, men are likely to resort to precisely this kind of effort to transcend history itself, that is, to find a timeless, 'deathless' dimension. Such things as the drug revolution among the young, and their general stress upon intense experience, or upon what could be called experiential radicalism—whether in politics, art, or life-style—all these may well be quests for new forms of experiential transcendence, quests that are greatly intensified by the other symbolic impairments brought about by nuclear weapons.

What I am suggesting in all this is that nuclear weapons alter and blur the boundaries of our psychological lives, of our symbolic space, in ways crucial to our thought, feelings, and actions.

The most extreme state of contemporary deformation is a pattern which may best be called 'nuclearism.' By this term I mean to suggest the passionate embrace of nuclear weapons as a solution to our anxieties (especially our anxieties concerning the weapons themselves), and as a means of restoring a lost sense of immortality. That is, one turns to the weapons, and to their power, as means of restoring boundaries. Nuclearism, then, is a secular religion, a total ideology in which grace, the mastery of death, is achieved by means of a new technological deity. This deity is seen as an all-powerful force, capable of both apocalyptic destruction and unlimited creation, and the nuclear believer, or nuclearist, allies himself to that force and feels compelled to expound the virtues of his god.

One's commitment to nuclearism, as in the case of any religion or sacralized idea-system, is likely to begin with some form of conversion experience—with an immersion in death anxiety, followed by a sense of rebirth and new world view. This was precisely what happened to many who witnessed the first atomic explosions. If one reads accounts of reactions to the Alamogordo test of July, 1945, one encounters such exclamations and images as "The sun can't hold a candle to it"; or, better known, "I am become death, the shatterer of worlds"; or, "This was the nearest to doomsday one can possibly imagine."

Now I am not suggesting that each of the scientists I have quoted became a convert to nuclearism, but rather that their apocalyptic exposure had elements of an end-of-the-world experience, and left a profound imprint of a symbolic death immersion. This imprint affected not only their inner lives from then on, but in many cases their choices, actions, and social commitments as well. A significant number of them chose to bear nuclear witness to what they had experienced, to warn the world about the new dangers so vividly revealed to them in the first detonations of the weapons they themselves had done so much to create. Others of course simply went about their professional work as if nothing had happened, though this required that they numb themselves to what they had witnessed in ways I shall try to make clear in a moment. And a few remained entranced by—bound to —the force, and took the path of nuclearism.

These problems have hardly been limited to scientists. One gets a sense of the apocalyptic tone of the more general American response to the early press reports following President Truman's announcement that an atomic bomb had been used on Hiroshima. An article in the New York *Herald Tribune* described the new force as "weird, incredible and somehow disturbing" and went on to say that "one forgets the effect on Japan or on the course of the war, as one senses the foundations of one's own universe trembling." Again, this is language very close to that which William James described as characteristic of religious conversion. Similarly, a witness of the earlier Alamogordo test explosion used terms such as "mighty thunder" and "great silence," and went on to say: "On that moment hung eternity. Time stood still . . . . One felt as though he had been privileged to witness the birth of the world." This is language suggesting a 'conversion in the desert,' once more the language of religious experience.

The same man, a science writer, used a similar tone nine years later in describing America's first airborne hydrogen bomb explosion, which took place in the northern Pacific in May, 1956. He spoke of "a gigantic pillar of fire," of a "cloud [which] rose and spread into the boiling mushroom at its top," and of a "sky . . . tinged by the rising sun to the east of it." He was, he said, "momentarily staggered by the thought of what the fireball and mushroom . . . would do to any of the world's great cities," but soon had "a second, more reassuring thought" which became "uppermost" in his mind, and which grew "ever more reassuring" over the years that followed. That thought was: "This great iridescent cloud and its mushroom top . . . is actually a protective umbrella, which will forever shield mankind everywhere against the threat of annihilation in any atomic war." He went on to describe "this rising supersun" as "the symbol of the dawn of a new era in which any sizable war had become impossible"—impossible because "This world-covering protective umbrella . . . will continue shielding us everywhere, until the time comes, as come it must, when mankind will be able to beat atomic swords into ploughshares, harnessing the vast power of the hydrogen in the world's oceans to bring an era of prosperity such as the world has never even dared dream about." And his conclusion: "To those who would have us stop our tests in the Pacific, I would therefore say, 'These tests, and others of improved models to come, serve as an effective substitute for war. History will record, I am sure, that World War III was fought and won on the Pacific proving ground in the Marshall Islands without the loss of a single life and without the slightest damage to any inhabited locality anywhere in the world.' "

What I want to stress here is the sequence of nuclear imagery from total annihilation to equally total—and comforting—protection. The deity is awesome, dreadful in its apocalyptic potential, but it is also the savior of mankind. The arbiter of immortality must of course be both.

Now, this same writer became a defender of the hydrogen bomb, and an enthusiast for "humanizing the hydrogen bomb" by eliminating from it much of the deadly irradiation. He welcomed the 'clean bomb' as a much more humane weapon—although it later developed that the 'clean bomb' was not so 'clean' after all. But significantly enough, when a third generation of nuclear weaponry, the neutron bomb, came along (if we consider the atomic bomb as the first generation, and the hydrogen bomb as the second generation) this same writer opposed it. He viewed the neutron bomb as a highly immoral weapon, as "a poison gas abhorrent to civilized humanity, a monster that rather than kill would, in the current nuclear jargon, juice its victims." And he condemned the entire effort to produce this new bomb.

Here we encounter what might be called 'nuclear backsliding.' That is, the nuclearist reaches a point beyond which he feels himself unable to go, beyond which he cannot inwardly sustain the moral structure of nuclearism. For him to go further with the rationalization of loathsome possibilities would threaten his entire ideological commitment to the weapons. One can speak of a kind of nuclear 'Kronstadt'—using the analogy of an event (the bloody suppression by the Soviet regime of a sailors' rebellion in 1921) that has come to symbolize the defection of the true believer from his cause. The extension of nuclearism becomes too grotesque, more than one can stomach, too laden with death guilt.

What I have been calling nuclearism, then, involves a search for grace and glory in which technical-scientific transcendence, apocalyptic destruction, national power, personal salvation, and committed individual identity—all these become bound up psychologically with the bomb. The weapon itself comes to usurp all of the pathways to symbolic immortality. Nuclearism can be particularly marked in scientists, politicians, and military men most closely involved with weaponry, but it is by no means confined to them. Rather, it is a general twentieth-century disease of power, a form of totalism of thought and consequences particularly tempting to contemporary man, both because of its technological idiom and its provision of a mode of symbolic immortality at a time when one is so desperately sought.

To some extent, anyone who inhabits a world in which nuclear weapons exist is himself enmeshed in nuclearism. That is why the general problem of coping with it is so great. Its malignant potential is unlimited. For nuclearism not only threatens the boundaries between man and his tools, but those between creativity and destruction, between communal development and communal annihilation, between species life and species death.

I want to speak of a last deformation of a somewhat different kind, not as extreme perhaps but even more widespread, that which I call 'psychic numbing.' In Hiroshima, a defense mechanism called forth by people exposed to the horrors of the bomb was simply to cease to feel, that is, to become psychologically desensitized. Virtually every survivor I spoke to told of some such psychological state at the time the bomb fell. They described being fully aware of what was going on around them, knowing that people were dying in horrible ways, but of simply losing their emotional involvement in it all. They used such phrases as "paralysis of the mind," or "I simply became insensitive to human death," and many others of an analogous kind. This form of psychic closing-off (a term for the acute process) or psychic numbing was necessary to Hiroshima survivors, as it is for anyone exposed to extreme catastrophe. It is a protection against overwhelming and unacceptable stimuli, and it is associated with an inner imagery that goes something like this: "If I feel nothing, then death is not taking place"; or, "If I feel nothing, I cannot be threatened by the death all around me"; or, "If I feel nothing, then I am not responsible for you or your death."

The difficulty was that the numbing process did not necessarily end when the danger was over. Survivors could undergo what is sometimes called 'miscarried repair.' They could continue to feel relatively numbed over weeks, months, even years of their lives subsequent to the catastrophe, as psychic numbing gave way to longer-range symptoms of despair and depression, or various forms of withdrawal and a generally constricted life pattern.

But I began to think of psychic numbing as a much more general problem, one always surrounded by the kind of paradox we observed in relationship to Hiroshima. For instance, a degree of psychic numbing is necessary for anyone who deals professionally with death. Certainly a surgeon must undergo what I would call selective and partial numbing in order not to feel the full consequences of success or failure in the technical task he has to perform. One can draw analogies with rescue workers of various kinds, and with physicians in general. And certainly in other forms of disaster, psychic numbing has been widespread, in, for instance, the apathy so often observed in victims. The paradox in all of these situations lies in the way in which the same process can serve as beneficial protection or harmful 'deadening,' depending upon its appropriateness and degree.

But I want to stress here the way in which psychic

numbing is called into play in relationship to the making, testing, and anticipated use of nuclear weapons. Indeed, so pervasive has psychic numbing become, much of it in relationship to these weapons, that, rather than the age of anxiety we could well speak of an Age of Numbing. To put the matter simply, one cannot afford to imagine what really happens at the other end of the weapon.

Concerning the atomic bomb, for instance, one could find evidence of psychic numbing in the scientists who created it and the way in which they looked upon what they were doing; in the behavior of the political leaders who made the decision to drop it, or at least failed to decide not to drop it; and in the pilots and crewmen who carried it to, and released it over, its target. When I say this, I am not name-calling, but attempting to illustrate a general phenomenon. In any case, I would stress the widespread, indeed universal, nuclear numbing affecting us today.

The nuclear-induced psychic numbing that I am talking about is more than a defense mechanism. It really amounts to a reorientation of the entire self, with a muting of overall response to the nuclear environment. It is another form of impairment to the symbolizing process, especially to that aspect of it which ordinarily harmonizes cognitive and emotional elements—what one knows and what one feels. Thus we can now speak of knowledge without feeling. We can also speak of a profound symbolic gap characteristic of our age, a gap between the capacity for technological violence on the one hand, and our much more limited capacity for moral imagination on the other.

Now these three deformations I have discussed—impaired symbolic immortality, nuclearism, and psychic numbing—

all include a breakdown of boundaries. These boundaries are largely symbolic ones, but they are crucial to our existence—to the decisions we make and the way that we live. Their breakdown has greatly contributed to a kind of cosmic distress.

It is not the sort of distress that can be overcome by any specific action or set of laws. Again I raise these issues in a spirit of psychological and historical confrontation. They are unpalatable matters but I believe that recognizing them is at least a first step toward ordering them, or rather, reordering ourselves in relationship to them. And further efforts at deepening our psychohistorical insight could in turn help us to create new kinds of political, institutional and legal structures appropriate to our unprecedented situation. We must desacralize the nuclear diety, for we can rid ourselves of it only by relegating it to the destructive material entity that it is. We can then reestablish necessary boundaries between man and his destructive tools, reclaim the psychic territory usurped by these weapons, and in the process reclaim ourselves.

SELF

The boundaries I have discussed so far have had to do with destruction and death. I want to turn now to another kind of boundary, by no means unrelated to those I have already spoken of, that of the self. Here, too, I believe we must call into question a number of conventional concepts. I have in mind especially those concepts which stress a precise demarcation, the kind of fixity and permanence of the self that is usually implied by such terms as 'character' and 'personality.' I think we require, in fact, a radical departure from this point of view in order to grasp the ever more significant elements of change and flux which characterize not only our external environment but our inner experience. And in this spirit, I have evolved a concept of 'Protean man'—named, of course, after that intriguing figure of Greek mythology renowned for his shape-shifting—in order to describe an emerging psychological style which I believe characteristic of much in contemporary life. I have done so as part of a continuing attempt to combine psychological and historical perspectives in connection with studies of Chinese, Japanese, and American experience.

The approach is related to psychoanalytic tradition. But it differs from that tradition in stressing the evolution of psychological forms, or what I call a formative perspective, in contrast to a purely analytic or atomizing one. It is also related to the concept of 'national character' as described in the early postwar years, especially by Margaret Mead and Ruth Benedict, and to others' concepts of 'social character' and of 'modal personality.' These older concepts are relevant, but often as a point of comparison or contrast, since my own historical stress moves away from the image of relatively fixed character, national or social. The work is very much in the spirit of such social and psychological theorists as David Riesman and Erik Erikson, who have also emphasized ways in which the inner life of individuals shapes itself in relationship to larger historical currents. Erikson's concept of identity has been, among other things, an effort to get away from the principle of fixity. I have been using the term 'self-process' to convey still more specifically the idea of flow, and of fluidity of boundaries.

For I think it quite possible that even the image of personal identity, insofar as it suggests inner stability and sameness, is derived from a vision of traditional culture in which man's relationship to his institutions and symbols is still relatively intact. And this, of course, is hardly the case today. (Even in traditional societies we cannot say that the boundaries of the self were sharply defined, since the individual tended to merge with precisely those institutions and symbols. What we can say is that the social constellation as a whole—made up of institutions, symbols, and of individual selves—had clear psychological and ethical contours, that is, relatively intact boundaries.) If we understand the self to be the person's symbol of his own organism, then, self-process refers to the continuous psychic re-creation of that symbol.

I originally came to this kind of emphasis in work in cultures quite removed from my own, studies I did of young (and not-so-young) Chinese and Japanese, but observations I could make on coming back to America convinced me that a very general process was taking place. I do not mean to suggest that everybody is becoming the same, or that a totally new 'world self' is taking shape. But I am suggesting that a new style of self-process is emerging everywhere. What this means is that more and more people are experiencing certain psychological processes in common, and that these, generally speaking, involve changing self-definitions, or at least blurring of perceptions of where self begins and ends. This shared style of self-process derives from what I see to be a three-way interplay responsible for the behavior of all human groups. This interplay includes, first, the psychobiological potential common to all mankind, that is, the universal dimension; second, those traits given special emphasis or style in a particular cultural tradition, the cultural or national-character emphasis; and third, that element related to modern (and especially contemporary) historical forces, the historical dimension. My general thesis is that the third factor, that of shared history, plays an increasingly important part in shaping the self-process.

My work with Chinese was done in Hong Kong, in connection with a study of the process of "thought reform" (or "brainwashing") as conducted in mainland China. I found that Chinese intellectuals of varying ages, whatever their experience with thought reform itself, had gone through an extraordinary set of what I at that time called identity fragments—of combinations of belief and emotional involvement—each of which they could readily abandon in favor of another. I remember the profound impression made upon me by the extraordinary history of one young man in particular: beginning as a 'filial son' or 'young master,' that elite status of an only son in an upper-class Chinese family; then feeling himself an abandoned and betrayed victim, as traditional forms collapsed during civil war and general chaos, and his father, for whom he was to long all his life, was separated from him by political and military duties; then a 'student activist' in rebellion against the traditional culture in which he had been so recently immersed (as well as against a Nationalist regime whose abuses he had personally experienced); leading him to Marxism and to strong emotional involvement in the Communist movement; then, because of remaining 'imperfections,' becoming a participant in a thought reform program for a more complete ideological conversion; but which, in his case, had the opposite effect, alienating him, so he came into conflict with the reformers and fled the country; then, in Hong Kong, struggling to establish himself as an 'anti-Communist writer'; after a variety of difficulties, finding solace and meaning in becoming a Protestant convert; and following that, still just thirty, apparently poised for some new internal (and perhaps external) move.

Even more dramatic were the shifts in self-process of a young Japanese whom I interviewed in Tokyo and Kyoto from 1960 to 1962. I shall mention one in particular as an extreme example of this Protean pattern, though there were many others who in various ways resembled him. Before the age of twenty-five he had been all of the following: a proper middle-class Japanese boy, brought up in a professional family within a well-established framework of dependency and obligation; then, due to extensive contact with farmers' and fishermen's sons brought about by wartime evacuation, a 'country boy' who was to retain what he described as a life-long attraction to the tastes of the common man; then, a fiery young patriot who "hated the Americans" and whose

older brother, a Kamikaze pilot, was saved from death only
by the war's end; then a youngster confused in his beliefs
after Japan's surrender, but curious about, rather than hos-
tile toward, American soldiers; soon an eager young exponent of democracy, caught up in the 'democracy boom'
which swept Japan; at the same time a youthful devotee of
traditional Japanese art—old novels, Chinese poems, ka-
buki and flower arrangement; during junior high and high
school, an all-round leader, outstanding in studies, student
self-government, and general social and athletic activities;
almost simultaneously, an outspoken critic of society at
large and of fellow students in particular for their narrow
careerism, on the basis of Marxist ideas current in Japanese
intellectual circles; yet also an English-speaking student,
which meant, in effect, being in still another vanguard and
having strong interest in things American; then, midway
through high school, experiencing what he called a "kind of
neurosis" in which he lost interest in everything he was
doing and, in quest of a "change in mood," took advantage
of an opportunity to become an exchange student for one
year at an American high school; became a convert to many
aspects of American life, including actually being baptized
as a Christian under the influence of a minister he admired
who was also his American 'father,' and returned to Japan
only reluctantly; as a 'returnee,' found himself in many
ways at odds with his friends and was accused by one of
"smelling like butter" (a traditional Japanese phrase for
Westerners or Westernized Japanese); therefore reim-
mersed himself in 'Japanese' experience—sitting on *tatami*,
indulging in quiet, melancholy moods, drinking tea, and so
on; then became a *rōnin*—in feudal days, a Samurai with-

out a master, now a student without a university—because
of failing his examinations for Tokyo University (a sort of
Harvard, Yale, Columbia, and Berkeley rolled into one),
and as is the custom spending the following year preparing
for the next round rather than attend a lesser institution;
once admitted, found little to interest him until becoming
an enthusiastic *Zengakuren* activist, with full embrace of its
ideal of 'pure communism' and a profound sense of fulfill-
ment in taking part in the planning and carrying out of student demonstrations; but when offered a high position in
the organization during his junior year, abruptly became an
ex-*Zengakuren* activist by resigning, because he felt he was
not suited for "the life of a revolutionary"; then an aimless
dissipator, as he drifted into a pattern of heavy drinking,
marathon mah-jongg games and affairs with bargirls; but
when the time came, had no difficulty gaining employment
with one of Japan's mammoth industrial organizations (and
one of the *bêtes noires* of his Marxist days) and embarking
upon the life of a young executive or *sarariman* (salaried
man)—in fact doing so with eagerness, careful preparation,
and relief, but at the same time having fantasies and dreams
of kicking over the traces, sometimes violently, and embarking upon a world tour (largely Hollywood-inspired) of
exotic and sophisticated pleasure-seeking.

Now this of course is a very rapid run-through of a young
man's life experiences. My aim is to show the flux in a series
of his identifications. The identifications vary greatly in
depth and intensity, in their general meaning for him. Nor
did each new identification require that earlier ones be totally surrendered. Further, there are important differences
between the Protean life-styles of the two young men dis-

cussed, and between each of them and their American counterparts, differences which have to do with cultural emphases, and which relate to what I referred to earlier as 'national character.' Yet such is the intensity of the shared aspects of historical experience that contemporary Chinese, Japanese, and American self-processes turn out to have striking points of convergence.

I would stress here two general historical developments as being of special importance for creating Protean man. The first of these is the world-wide sense of what I called *historical,* or *psychohistorical* dislocation, the break in the sense of connection men have long felt with vital and nourishing symbols of their cultural traditions—symbols revolving around family, idea systems, religions, and the life cycle in general. In our contemporary world, one perceives these traditional symbols as irrelevant, burdensome, or even inactivating, and yet one cannot avoid carrying them within, or having one's self-process profoundly affected by them.

The second large historical tendency is the *flooding of imagery* produced by the extraordinary flow of post-modern cultural influences over mass communication networks. I would greatly stress the role of mass media in creating Protean man. The images they convey cross over all boundaries, local and national, and permit each individual everywhere to be touched by everything, but at the same time often cause him to be overwhelmed by superficial messages and undigested cultural elements, by headlines and by endless partial alternatives in every sphere of life. In other words, as an individual one can maintain no clear boundaries. And the alternatives contained in the endless flow of images are universally and simultaneously shared, if not as courses of action, at least in the form of significant inner possibilities.

One could add a third important historical dimension: that which I spoke of in the previous two chapters, the impact of nuclear weapons and the kinds of threat to self and to the symbolism of self associated with the breakdown of boundaries of destruction. This, too, has great importance for Protean man.

Now, we know from Greek mythology that Proteus was able to change his shape with relative ease from wild boar to lion to dragon to fire to flood. What he found difficult, and would not do unless seized and chained, was to commit himself to a single form, a form most his own, and carry out his function of prophecy. We can say the same of Protean man, but we must keep in mind his possibilities as well as his difficulties.

The Protean style of self-process, then, is characterized by an interminable series of experiments and explorations, some shallow, some profound, each of which can readily be abandoned in favor of still new, psychological quests. This pattern resembles, in many ways, what Erik Erikson has called "identity diffusion" or "identity confusion," and the impaired psychological functioning which these terms suggest can be very much present. But I want to stress that this Protean style is by no means pathological as such, and in fact may be one of the functional patterns necessary to life in our times. I would emphasize that it extends to all areas of human experience—to political as well as to sexual behavior, to the holding and promulgating of ideas, and to the general organization of lives. To grasp this style, then, we must alter our judgments concerning what is psychologically disturbed or pathological, as opposed to adaptive or even innovative.

I would like to suggest a few illustrations of the Protean style, as expressed in America and Europe, drawn both from my own psychotherapeutic work with patients, and from observations on various forms of literature and art.

One patient of mine, a gifted young teacher, referred to himself as "wearing a number of masks" which he could put on or take off. He asked the question, "Is there, or should there be, one face which should be authentic?" He wasn't really sure, and found parallels to this in literature, in which, he noted, there were representations of "every kind of crime, every kind of sin." And then he added: "For me, there's not a single act I cannot imagine myself committing." He went on to compare himself to an actor on the stage, who, as he put it, "performs with a certain kind of polymorphous versatility," and here he was of course referring, somewhat mockingly, to Freud's well-known phrase, "polymorphous perversity" for diffusely inclusive and, in a way also Protean, infantile sexuality. And he went on to ask: "Which is the real person, so far as an actor is concerned? Is he more real when performing on the stage, or when he is at home? I tend to think that for people who have these many, many masks, there is no home. Is it a futile gesture for the actor to try to find his real face?" Here he was asking a very fundamental question, one in fact at issue throughout this chapter. I would add that while he was by no means a happy man, neither was he incapacitated. And although he certainly had considerable strain with his "polymorphous versatility," it could be said that as a teacher and a thinker, and in some ways as a man, he was served rather well by it. In fact, I would claim that polymorphous versatility of one kind or another is becoming increasingly prominent in contemporary life.

In present-day American literature, Saul Bellow is notable for the Protean men he has created. In *The Adventures of Augie March,* one of his earlier novels, we meet a picaresque hero with an impressive talent for adapting himself to divergent social worlds. Augie himself says: "I touched all sides, and nobody knew where I belonged. I had no good idea of that myself." And a young English critic, Tony Tanner, comments further: "Augie indeed celebrates the self, but he can find nothing to do with it." Tanner also goes on to describe Bellow's more recent Protean hero, Herzog, as "a representative modern intelligence, swamped with ideas, metaphysics and values, and surrounded by messy facts. It labours to cope with them all."

One can find various continental parallels, perhaps especially in that distinguished French representative of the Protean style, Jean-Paul Sartre, and I refer both to his life and his work. I think it is because of Protean traits of the kind that I have been suggesting that Sartre strikes us as such an embodiment of twentieth-century man. Sartre's thought flows around impediments, over barriers, and past boundaries. An American critic, Theodore Solotaroff, captured this quality of Sartre when he referred to his fundamental assumption that "there is no such thing as even a relatively fixed sense of self, ego or identity—rather, there is only the subjective mind in motion in relationship to that which it confronts." Sartre himself, in fact, says almost the same thing when he refers to human consciousness as "a sheer ac-

tivity transcending towards objects," and "a great empti-
ness, a wind blowing toward objects." Now these may be
overstatements on the part of both men, but I don't think it
likely that this kind of overstatement would have been made
prior to the last thirty years or so.

Solotaroff further characterizes Sartre as "constantly on
the go, hurrying from point to point, subject to subject;
fiercely intentional, his thought occupies, fills and distends
his material as he endeavours to lose and find himself in his
encounters with other lives, disciplines, books, and situations." Here we have an image of repeated, autonomously
willed death and rebirth of the self, an image very central to
the Protean style. It becomes associated with themes of
fatherlessness, and these are very important for Sartre also,
as he makes clear in one rather interesting section of his au-
tobiography, *The Words*. Sartre treats his own state of fatherlessness with a characteristic tone of serious self-mockery:
"There is no good father, that's the rule. Don't lay the
blame on men but on the bond of paternity, which is rotten.
To beget children, nothing better; to have them, what iniq-
uity! Had my father lived, he would have laid on me at full
length and would have crushed me." And he goes on: "I left
behind me a young man who did not have time to be my father, and who could now be my son. Was it a good thing or
bad? I don't know. But I readily subscribe to the verdict of
an eminent psychoanalyst: I have no Superego." One
should note Sartre's image of interchangeability of father
and son—of, as he puts it, "a young man who did not have
time to be my father, and who could now be my son,"
which in a literal sense refers to the age of his father's
death, but more symbolically suggests an extension of the

Protean style to intimate family relationships. This sort of reversal becomes more and more necessary in a rapidly changing world in which sons must constantly teach their fathers new things, which they, the fathers, as older people cannot possibly know.

Now here we see a fundamental breakdown in the boundaries of mentorship and authority—not only between father and son, but also between teacher and student, master and disciple, the old and the young, the experienced and the neophyte, and so on all through society. This kind of breakdown, based as it is in shifts in knowledgeability, has enormous consequences throughout the world. And I shall return in subsequent chapters to related issues surrounding the interplay of knowledgeability and authority.

But to get back to Sartre, the allegedly psychoanalytic verdict of an absent superego could well be misleading, especially if we make a simple equation between superego and susceptibility to guilt. What has actually disappeared in Sartre, and in Protean man in general, is the classic superego, the internalization of clearly defined criteria of right and wrong, transmitted within a particular culture by parents to their children. Freud's original description of the superego, in other words, referred to stable moral and psychological structures much more characteristic of traditional cultures than of our own. Indeed, Protean man requires freedom from precisely that kind of superego—he requires a symbolic form of fatherlessness—in order to carry out his explorations. But rather than being free of guilt, we shall soon see that his guilt takes on a different form from that of his predecessors. And here I am in disagreement with the idea, put forth from many quarters, that contemporary man is losing his sense of guilt.

There are many other representations of Protean man among contemporary novelists. One need only think of the 'Beat Generation' writing, such as Jack Kerouac's *On The Road* and the work of a very gifted successor to that generation, J. P. Donlevy, especially his early novel *The Ginger Man*. One thinks also of the work of John Barth, as well as of various more recent writings influenced by the hippie life-style. Also, the work of many European novelists comes to mind, particularly that of Günter Grass, whose book, *The Tin Drum,* is a breathtaking evocation of prewar Polish-German, wartime German, and postwar German environments, in which the protagonist combines Protean adaptability with a kind of perpetual physical-mental strike against any change at all. Grass thus provides us with both sides of the Protean dilemma.

In the visual arts, perhaps the most important of postwar movements has been aptly named Action Painting to convey its stress upon process rather than fixed completion. And a more recent, and I think psychologically related, movement in sculpture, called Kinetic Art, goes further. According to Jean Tinguely, one of its leading practitioners: "Artists are putting themselves in rhythm with their time, in contact with their epoch, especially with permanent and perpetual movement." This statement may reflect the feelings of many artists not necessarily associated with the Kinetic Art movement.

As revolutionary as any style or approach is the stress upon innovation per se, which now dominates so much of painting. One thinks especially of the recent vogue of Destructive Art, the making of paintings or pieces of sculpture only to be physically destroyed. There can be nothing more Protean than that.

But I have frequently heard artists, themselves at one time considered radical innovators, complain bitterly of the current standards dictating something in the nature of "innovation is all." What they are complaining about, of course, is a turnover in art movements so rapid as to discourage the idea of holding still long enough to develop any particular style. The moral here perhaps is that, in creative work as in living, the loss of boundaries is a mixed blessing. But, concerning art in particular, much more careful distinctions shall have to be made about the nature and possibilities of the Protean style. My impression is that artists themselves have hardly begun to explore these possibilities.

We can also learn much here from film stars. I think of Marcello Mastroianni who, when asked whether he agreed with *Time* magazine's characterization of him as "the neo-capitalist hero," gave the following answer: "In many ways, yes, but I don't think I'm any kind of hero, neo-capitalist or otherwise. If anything I'm an *anti*-hero, or at most a *non*-hero. *Time* said I had the frightened, characteristically twentieth-century look, with a spine made of plastic napkin rings. I accepted this, because modern man is that way, and being a product of my time, and an artist, I can represent him. If humanity were all one piece, I would be considered a weakling." Mastroianni accepts his destiny as Protean man. He seems to realize that there are certain advantages to having a spine made of plastic napkin rings, or at least that in some ways it is an appropriate kind of spine to have these days. The image here is that of 'backbone' (representing strength, courage, and will) rendered flimsy but malleable, and possibly even having a certain amount of toughness in weakness.

John Cage, the composer, is an extreme exponent of the Protean style, both in his music and in his sense of all of us as listeners. In a letter he wrote to *The Village Voice* he said: "Nowadays everything happens at once and our souls are conveniently electronic, omniattentive." Now this is, of course, a McLuhan-like comment, but what I wish to stress particularly is the idea of omniattention, the sense of contemporary man as having the possibility of 'receiving' and 'taking in' everything. In attending, as in being, nothing is 'off limits.' All this is not only a matter of a 'global village,' though I think McLuhan's term is an apt one, but also of a confused, responsive, increasingly knowledgeable and in many ways creative, but symbolically unhinged villager. And I think it is this dimension of the man in the village, or one might say, of the mind of the villager, that McLuhan does not deal with.

Now, one has to grant that one can observe in contemporary man a tendency which seems to be precisely the opposite of the Protean style I have been describing. I refer here to the closing off of identity, the constriction of self-process, to a straight-and-narrow specialization in psychological as well as in intellectual life, and to reluctance to let in any extraneous influence. This kind of 'one-dimensional' self-process, however, I would see as having an essentially reactive or compensatory quality. In this it differs from earlier characteriological styles it may seem to resemble, such as Riesman's inner-directed man, and still earlier patterns in

traditional society. For these were direct outgrowths of societies which then existed, and were therefore in harmony
with those societies, while the constricted self-process that I
am describing requires continuous psychological work to
fend off Protean influences which are always abroad.

Here I would say that Marcuse's idea of 'one-dimensional
man' is true only to a limited degree. I don't think that such
a man is directly molded by a suffocating society (as Marcuse claims), although much in our society may indeed en-
courage his development. Rather I see him as a kind of
fearful reaction to what he perceives to be a threat
emanating from the Protean style. In this sense, I see two
related difficulties in Marcuse's style of analysis.

First, I believe he confuses a large general social mechanism, which he calls "advanced industrial society," with the
inner psychological experience of individual man—ignor-
ing the symbolic dislocations which man *brings* to his advanced industrial society. Man does not come to it naked,
so to speak. Saying the same thing in another way, I think
that Marcuse confuses man's social structure with his symbolic life. However suffocating advanced industrial society
may be, in its absence of symbolic coherence it can often be
perceived as formless. So we can speak of a paradox here,
in which society is often perceived as having a 'formless totality,' as being suffocating and monolithic but at the same
time lacking authentic institutional or symbolic form.

The second difficulty in Marcuse's views has to do with his
vision of society itself. Advanced industrial society, in my
opinion, is by no means as integrated a mechanism as he describes. It is neither as stable nor static a constellation as he
makes it out to be. We have in fact been witnessing indica-

tions of increasing vulnerability, of susceptibility to influence and possibly to breakdown, within advanced industrial societies throughout the world.

Concerning these and other questions, what I am calling the Protean style has broad, if as yet unclear implications for the nature and direction of society in our advanced industrial age. These implications require careful investigation, quite beyond the preliminary statement I am making now.

Protean man has a particular relationship to the holding of ideas, which I think has great significance for the politics, religion, and general intellectual life of the future. Just as elements of the self can be experimented with and readily altered, so can idea systems and ideologies be embraced, modified, let go of and reembraced, all with a new ease that stands in sharp contrast to the inner struggle we have in the past associated with these shifts. Until relatively recently, no more than one major ideological shift was likely to occur in a lifetime, and that one would be long remembered as a very significant inner individual turning point accompanied by profound soul-searching and conflict. But today, it is not so unusual to encounter several such shifts accomplished relatively painlessly within a year, or even a month, whether in politics, aesthetic values, or style of living. Among many groups the rarity is the man who has gone through life holding firmly to a single ideological vision.

In one sense, this tendency is related to the 'end of ideology' spoken of by Daniel Bell, since Protean man is incapable of maintaining an unquestioning allegiance to the large ideologies and Utopian thought of the nineteenth and early twentieth centuries. One must be very cautious, however, about speaking of the end of anything, especially ideology, and one also encounters in Protean man what I would call strong ideological hunger. He is starved for ideas and feelings that can give coherence to his world, though here too his taste is toward new combinations. And while he is by no means without yearning for the absolute, what he finds most acceptable are images of a more fragmentary nature than those of the ideologies of the past. And these images, limited and fleeting though they may be, can have enormous influence on his psychological life. Thus political and religious movements, as they confront Protean man, are likely to have much less difficulty convincing him to alter previous convictions than they do providing him with a set of beliefs which can command his allegiance for more than a brief experimental interlude. The problem is to build structures, to create boundaries, but not just any structures or any boundaries, and not just at any given historical moment. Here one must keep in mind Protean man's allergy to that which strikes him as inauthentic.

And bound up with his flux in emotions and beliefs is a profound inner sense of absurdity which finds expression in a tone of mockery. Absurdity and mockery are central to Protean man, and are related to a perception of surrounding activities and beliefs as strange and inappropriate. They stem from a breakdown of a fundamental kind in the relationship between inner and outer worlds—that is, in the sense of symbolic integrity—and are part of the pattern of psychohistorical dislocation I mentioned earlier. For if we view man as primarily a symbol-forming organism, we must recognize that he has constant need of a meaningful inner formulation of self and world, in which his actions, and even his impulses, have some kind of 'fit' with the 'outside' as he perceives it.

The sense of absurdity, of course, has a considerable modern tradition, and has been discussed by such writers as Camus as a function of man's spiritual homelessness and inability to find any meaning in traditional belief systems. But absurdity and mockery have taken much more extreme form in the post-World War II world, and have in fact become a prominent part of a universal life-style.

In American life, absurdity and mockery are everywhere. Perhaps their most vivid expression can be found in such areas as Pop Art and the more general burgeoning of 'pop culture.' Important here is the complex stance of the pop artist (and his cultural successors) toward the objects he depicts. On the one hand he embraces the materials of the everyday world, celebrates and even exalts them—boldly asserting his creative return to representational art (in active rebellion against the previously reigning nonobjective school), and his psychological return to the 'real world' of *things*. On the other hand, everything he touches he mocks. 'Thingness' is pressed to the point of caricature. He is indeed artistically reborn as he moves freely among the physical and symbolic materials of his environment, but mockery is his birth certificate and his passport. This kind of duality of approach is formalized in the stated 'duplicity' of Camp, a poorly defined aesthetic in which (among other things) all varieties of mockery converge under the guiding influence of the homosexual's subversion of a heterosexual world.

Also relevant are a group of expressions in current slang, some of them derived originally from jazz. The 'dry mock' has replaced the dry wit; one refers to a segment of life experience as a 'bit,' 'bag,' 'caper,' 'game' (or 'con game'), 'scene,' 'show,' 'scenario,' or, most significant of all, 'put-on'; and one seeks to 'make the scene' (or 'make it'), 'beat the system' or 'pull it off'—or else one 'cools it' ('plays it cool') or 'cops out.' The thing to be experienced, in other words, is too absurd to be taken at its face value; one must either keep most of the self aloof from it, or if not one must lubricate the encounter with mockery. Such lubrication is a means of easing the crossing-over of boundaries that can no longer be respected.

A similar spirit seems to pervade literature and social action alike. What is best termed a 'literature of mockery' has come to dominate fiction and other forms of writing on an international scale. Again Günter Grass's *The Tin Drum* comes to mind, and is probably the greatest single example of this literature—a work, I believe, which will eventually be appreciated as much as a general evocation of contemporary man as of the particular German experience with Nazism. In this country the divergent group of novelists known as 'black humorists' also fit into the general category —related as they are to a trend in the American literary consciousness which R. W. B. Lewis has called a "savagely comical apocalypse" or a "new kind of ironic literary form and disturbing vision, the joining of the dark thread of apocalypse with the nervous detonations of satiric laughter." For it is precisely death itself, and particularly threats of the contemporary apocalypse, that Protean man ultimately mocks.

The relationship of mockery to political and social action has been less apparent, but is, I would claim, equally significant. There is more than coincidence in the fact that the

SELF 57

largest American student uprising of recent decades, the
Berkeley Free Speech Movement of 1964, was followed immediately by a "Filthy Speech Movement." While the object
of the Filthy Speech Movement—achieving free expression
of forbidden language, particularly of four-letter words
—can be viewed as a serious one, the predominant effect,
even in the matter of names, was that of a mocking caricature of the movement which preceded it. But if mockery can undermine protest, it can also enliven it. There have
been signs of craving for it in such major American expressions of protest as black power, opposition to the war in
Vietnam, and student rebellion. A certain chord can be
struck by the comedian Dick Gregory, by satirical anti-
war skits and parodies, by the graffiti of the Paris uprisings
of 1968 or the "Up against the wall, motherfucker" slogan
of Columbia students, that revives the flagging attention of
protesters becoming gradually bored with the repetition of
their 'straight' slogans and goals. And on an international
scale, I would say that, during the past decade, Russian intellectual life has been enriched by a leavening spirit of
mockery—against which the Chinese leaders are now, in
the 'purifications' of the Cultural Revolution, fighting a vigorous but ultimately losing battle.

Closely related to the sense of absurdity and the spirit of
mockery is another characteristic of Protean man which can
be called 'suspicion of counterfeit nurturance.' Involved
here is a severe conflict of dependency, a core problem of
Protean man. I first began to think of the concept several
years ago while working with survivors of the atomic bomb
in Hiroshima. I found that these survivors both felt themselves in need of special help, and resented whatever help

was offered them because they equated it with weakness and inferiority. In considering the matter more generally, I found this equation of nurturance with a threat to autonomy to be a major theme of contemporary life. The increased dependency needs, resulting from the breakdown of traditional institutions, lead Protean man to seek out replacements wherever he can find them. The large organizations (government, business, academic, etc.) to which he turns, and which contemporary society more and more holds out as a substitute for traditional institutions, present an ambivalent threat to his autonomy in one way; and the intense individual relationships in which he seeks to anchor himself in another. Both are therefore likely to be perceived as counterfeit. But the obverse side of this tendency is an expanding sensitivity to the inauthentic, which may be just beginning to exert its general creative force on man's behalf.

Technology (and technique in general), together with science, has special significance for Protean man. Technical achievement of any kind can be strongly embraced to combat inner tendencies toward diffusion, and to transcend feelings of absurdity and conflicts over counterfeit nurturance. The image of science itself, however, as the ultimate power behind technology and, to a considerable extent, behind contemporary thought in general, becomes much more difficult to cope with. Only in certain underdeveloped countries can one find, in relatively pure form, those expectations of scientific-Utopian deliverance from all human want and conflict which were characteristic of eighteenth- and nineteenth-century Western thought. Protean man retains some of this Utopian imagery, but he finds it increasingly undermined by massive disillusionment. More and more he calls forth the other side of the God-devil polarity generally applied to science, and sees it as a purveyor of total destructiveness. This kind of profound ambivalence creates for him the most extreme psychic paradox: the very force he still feels to be his liberator from the heavy burdens of past irrationality also threatens him with absolute annihilation, even extinction. As part of his counterattack against science and technology he may seem to embrace precisely that 'past irrationality.' But he is much more involved in a technological-scientific universe than he realizes, even in his language and images. Yet this very paradox could well give rise to imaginative efforts to achieve new relationships between science and man, and new visions of science itself. We may well in fact be on the verge of these new visions.

I suggested before that Protean man was not free of guilt. He indeed suffers from it considerably, but often without awareness of what is causing his suffering. For his is a form of hidden guilt: a vague but persistent kind of self-condemnation related to the symbolic disharmonies I have described, a sense of having no outlet for his loyalties and no symbolic structure for his achievements. This is the guilt of social breakdown, and it includes various forms of historical and racial guilt experienced by whole nations and peoples, both by the privileged and the abused. Rather than a clear feeling of evil or sinfulness, it takes the form of a nagging sense of unworthiness all the more troublesome for its lack of clear origin.

Protean man experiences similarly vague constellations of anxiety and resentment. These too have origin in symbolic impairments and are particularly tied in with suspicion of counterfeit nurturance. Often feeling himself uncared for, even abandoned, Protean man responds with diffuse fear and anger. But he can neither find a good cause for the former, nor a consistent target for the latter. He nonetheless cultivates his anger because he finds it more serviceable than anxiety, because there are plenty of targets of one kind or another beckoning, and because even moving targets are better than none. His difficulty is that focused indignation is as hard for him to sustain as is any single identification or conviction. In his discomforts and even his symptoms he experiences the same kind of formlessness, together with flexibility and search, that characterizes the rest of his psychological experience.

Involved in all of these patterns is a profound psychic struggle with the idea of change itself. For here too Protean man finds himself ambivalent in the extreme. He is profoundly attracted to the idea of making all things, including himself, totally new—to the 'mode of transformation.' But he is equally drawn to an image of a mythical past of perfect harmony and prescientific wholeness, to the 'mode of restoration.' Moreover, beneath his transformationism is nostalgia, and beneath his restorationism is his fascinated attraction to contemporary forms and symbols. Constantly balancing these elements midst the extraordinary, rapid change surrounding his own life, the nostalgia is pervasive, and can be one of his most explosive and dangerous emotions. This longing for a 'Golden Age' of absolute oneness, prior to individual and cultural separation or delineation, not only sets the tone for the restoration of the politically rightist antagonists of history: the still-extant Emperor-worshiping assassins in Japan, the Colons in France, and the John Birchites and Wallaceites in the

United States. It also, in more disguised form, energizes that transformationist totalism of the Left which courts violence, and is even willing to risk nuclear violence, in a similarly elusive quest.

Following upon all that I have said are radical impairments to the symbolism of transition within the life cycle— the *rites de passage* surrounding birth, entry into adulthood, marriage, and death. Whatever rites remain seem shallow, inappropriate, fragmentary. Protean man cannot take them seriously, and often seeks to improvise new ones with whatever contemporary materials he has available, including cars and drugs. One need only think of ceremonials connected with hippie weddings, Yippie levitations, or Hindu incantations, to mention a few of the more exotic examples of what is really a general trend in ceremonial innovation, especially among the young. Perhaps the central impairment here is that of symbolic immortality (as described in Chapter II)—of the universal need for imagery of connection predating and extending beyond the individual life span, whether the idiom of this immortality is biological (living on through children and grandchildren), theological (through a life after death), natural (*in* nature itself which outlasts all), or creative (through what man makes and does). Not only is this sense of immortality threatened by nuclear weapons (Who can be certain of living on through children and grandchildren, through teachings or kindnesses?), but also by simple historical velocity—the speed of social change—which subverts the idioms (notably the theological) in which it has traditionally been maintained. As I suggested earlier, Protean man is left with two paths to symbolic immortality which he tries to cultivate, sometimes pleasurably and sometimes desperately: the natural mode (also under some threat) and the mode of 'experiential transcendence,' within which he not only embraces chemical aids to 'expanded consciousness,' but also the 'community high' of group living and political action. And indeed all revolutions may be thought of, at bottom, as innovations in the struggle for immortality, as new combinations of old modes.

Three questions about Protean man, each rather fundamental, readily arise. Is Protean man always a *young* man? Is he really a *new* man, or merely a resurrection of a type familiar from the past? And midst his fluidity, what, if anything, remains stable? To which I would answer, very briefly, as follows. The fluctuating pattern I described is indeed most prominent in the young (late teens and early twenties), but for the rest of us to assume that we are totally immune from it would seem to me to be a great mistake. My contention, in fact, is that Protean man inhabits us all. We all live in contemporary society, and are all in greater or lesser degree exposed to the forces I have mentioned. Although the pattern is most characteristic of advanced, affluent societies, even those in non-affluent, economically backward societies are by no means free of them. And although men resembling Protean man have undoubtedly existed in earlier historical periods that were, like our own, notably 'out of joint,' the extremity of recent historical developments has rendered him a much more discrete and widespread entity. That is what permits us to stress his emergence. Concerning his stability, it is true that much within him must remain constant in order to make possible his psychological flux. I would include here certain enduring

elements in the mother-child relationship, various consist-
encies in style (including elements of mockery and the
sense of absurdity, approaches to individual and group
relationships, and a generally aesthetic emphasis), as well
as the stabilizing aspect of constant anticipation of change
itself. The whole stability-change issue badly needs general
psychological reevaluation, especially in regard to the kinds
of significant change that can take place within a person while much else remains constant.

We may say then that young adults individually, and
youth movements collectively, express most vividly the psychological themes of Protean man. But we may also say that
Protean man's affinity for the young, his being metaphori-
cally and psychologically so young in spirit, has to do with
his never-ceasing quest for imagery of rebirth. He seeks
such imagery of rebirth from all sources, from ideas, tech-
niques, religions, and political systems, from mass movements and of course from drugs, or from special individuals
of his own kind—that is, from fellow Protean voyagers—
whom he sees as possessing that problematic gift of his
namesake, the gift of prophecy. The dangers inherent in the
quest seem hardly to require emphasis. What perhaps needs
most to be kept in mind is the general principle that renewal
on a large scale, wherever it may occur, is impossible to
achieve without forays into danger, destruction, and negativ-
ity. The principle of death and rebirth is as valid psycho-
historically as it is mythologically. And the direction of
Protean man's prophecy lies in new, fluid, threatening, liberating, confusing, and revitalizing personal boundaries.

REVOLUTION

Given such shifts in the boundaries of destruction, of death and life, and of self, we can hardly be surprised that the issue of revolution becomes a paramount one in our age. In this chapter I shall focus my discussion upon one particular experience with revolution: that of the Chinese Communist movement, and especially of its extraordinary leader, Mao Tse-tung, as manifested recently in the extraordinary events surrounding the Great Proletarian Cultural Revolution.

The best way I know to begin the discussion is to quote a simple and brief Chinese Communist slogan: "May the revolutionary regime stay red for ten thousand generations." Now the slogan is not a particularly remarkable one. It is in the spirit of many Chinese responses to heroic individuals and groups, Communist or otherwise, and it is a version of the universal toast to a long life. But if one looks at the slogan more carefully, one notes that the long life proposed is not for an individual, but for a regime. It is not even for the regime itself so much as for the 'redness' or revolutionary purity of that regime ("May the revolutionary regime stay *red*")—and for a purity that is not only long-lived, but virtually eternal ("that endures for ten thousand generations"). We are dealing, then, both with the boundaries of revolution and with the relationship of those boundaries to the question of immortality.

I chose the title "Revolutionary Immortality" for my recent study of Mao Tse-tung and the Chinese Cultural Revolution as a way of suggesting a fundamental issue that confronts all revolutions, and one which has bearing on man's general struggles with continuity and perpetuation.

I believe that we require a large framework of this kind in order to begin to make sense of the overwhelming events in China during 1966 and 1967 in association with the Great Proletarian Cultural Revolution: the dramatic emergence of militant and, at moments, all-powerful new groups, such as the Red Guards and the Revolutionary Rebels, with their campaigns of purification and vilification; the unprecedentedly undiplomatic verbal and physical abuse accorded various foreign diplomats; and the still more startling attacks upon Party leaders, along with general undermining of Party authority, culminating in violence and confusion of such magnitude as to suggest at times complete national chaos and civil war.

Now the explanation usually put forth for these vast events is that of a 'power struggle.' The implication is that this designation, together with a few comments about political rivalries, explains all. Sometimes, the explanation reverts to the state of Mao's physical or mental health as the key to everything taking place. And in Hong Kong in particular, I encountered articulate (even passionate) defenders of the point of view that Mao was in excellent health, severely ill, senile, mad, or dead. Important to both of these explanations, I think, is their neglect of larger historical and psychological forces.

There have, of course, been much more thoughtful explanations as well. These have stressed such factors as China's (and especially Mao's) 'Yenan Syndrome' or 'Complex,' the nostalgia for the heroic revolutionary methods and achievements of days gone by; China's abrupt loss of a comfortable relationship to her own cultural past; her sense of mounting threat from the outside, especially from America's intervention in Vietnam; and her undergoing a kind of 'Protestant-Catholic dispute' between evangelical reawakening and established bureaucratic compromise. All of these interpretations contain considerable truth, and the first in particular illuminates much of what has been occurring. But we have lacked a general perspective within which to comprehend both psychological motives and historical context—that is, a *psychohistorical* framework.

I propose such a framework, however tentative and precarious, because I believe it can reveal much about motivations behind and relationships between seemingly unfathomable and disjointed events, and at the same time possibly contribute to the general understanding of such upheavals, wherever they may occur. My goal is not to reduce the vast canvas of the Cultural Revolution to a set of individual-psychological observations. Rather, I wish to suggest a theoretical perspective which, while unitary, is also open and broadly inclusive. And in stressing shifting symbols and forms in the interplay of the individual with the collective, I see these as part of—not as an explanatory replacement for—the very important political, economic, and ideological struggles occurring.

I should like to suggest that much of what has been taking place in China recently can be understood as a quest for revolutionary immortality. By revolutionary immortality I mean a shared sense of participating in permanent revolutionary ferment, and of transcending individual death by 'living on' indefinitely within this continuing revolution. Some such vision has been present in all revolutions and was directly expressed in Trotsky's ideological principle of "permanent revolution" (even if other things were also meant by this term); but it has taken on unprecedented intensity in present-day Chinese Communist experience.

Central to this point of view is the concept of symbolic immortality I have described in earlier chapters—man's need for a *sense* of immortality as a form of connectedness with prior and future people and events. While this may at first seem a rather abstract approach to the passions and actions of old revolutionaries and young followers, I believe that only by recognizing such life-and-death components of the revolutionary psyche can we begin to comprehend precisely these passions and actions.

Applying these modes of symbolic immortality to the revolutionary, we may say that he becomes part of a vast 'family' reaching back to what he perceives to be the historical beginnings of his revolution and extending infinitely into the future. This socially created 'family' tends to replace the biological one as a mode of immortality; moreover, it can itself take on an increasingly biological quality, as, over the generations, revolutionary identifications become blended with national, cultural, and racial ones. The revolutionary denies theology as such, but embraces a secular Utopia through images closely related to the spiritual conquest of death and even to an afterlife. His revolutionary 'works' are all important, and only to the extent that he can perceive them as enduring can he achieve a measure of acceptance of his own eventual death. The natural world to which he allies himself is one that must be transformed by revolution while continuing to contain all that revolution creates. And his experiential transcendence can approach that of religious mystics, as a glance at some of the younger participants in China's Cultural Revolution confirms.

What all this suggests, then, is that the essence of the 'power struggle' taking place in China, as of all such 'power struggles,' is power over death. It also suggests that revolution itself is centrally concerned with the boundaries of individual and group existence.

It is impossible to know Mao's exact physical or mental state. But let us assume, on the basis of evidence we have, that the seventy-six-year-old (born December 26th, 1893) man has generally been vigorous, that he has experienced rather severe illness in recent years, and that he has always been a man of strong revolutionary passions. We can go a bit further, however, especially on the basis of a valuable interview with him conducted by Edgar Snow, perhaps the American who over the years has been closest to Mao, in January 1965.

During that interview, Mao made several references to his "getting ready to see God" (using the theological idiom somewhat wryly, as Snow noted). He also spoke of his amazing sequence of survivals in the face of the repeated deaths of so many close family members and equally close revolutionary comrades—the two categories of people more or less merging in his imagery—including several very narrow escapes in which men standing right next to him were killed.

In these ways and other ways Mao is surely the survivor *par excellence*. He is the hero of a truly epic story of revolutionary survival, that of the Long March of 1934-1935, in which it is believed that more than eighty percent of the original group perished along a six-thousand-mile trek, in order that the remainder, and the Revolution itself, might stay alive. To transcend his guilt over remaining alive while others die, the survivor must be able to render significant the death immersions he has experienced—and in Mao's case, done much to bring about. This kind of survivor formulation (as I suggested in Chapter I) faces both ways: justification of the past, and contribution to the future. Thus for a man in Mao's position, of his age and special commitments, the affirmation of a sense of immortality becomes crucial. The overwhelming threat is not so much death itself as the suggestion that his 'revolutionary works' will not endure.

We sense the passion behind his apparent calm as he goes on, during that same interview, to describe what he calls the "two possibilities" for the future: the first, "the continued development of the revolution toward Communism"; and the second, "that youth could negate the Revolution and give a poor performance: make peace with imperialism, bring the remnants of the Chiang Kai-shek clique back to the Mainland and take a stand beside the small percentage of counter-revolutionaries still in the country." The first is an image of continuous life; the second of death and extinction, of impaired immortality.

Mao's ultimate dread, the image of extinction which stalks him, is the death of the revolution. And when he speaks of the possible "poor performance" of the young, his overriding concern is that the immortal revolutionary legacy will be squandered, that in such unknowing hands, the sacred thing itself—the Revolution—could be abused, neglected, permitted to die. Such 'historical death' can, for the revolutionary, represent an 'end of the world,' an ultimate deformation and 'de-symbolization.'

During the Cultural Revolution (and of course before

that), Maoists have repeatedly called forth certain specific images to suggest the danger of the death of the revolution. These images include 'American imperialism,' 'feudalism,' 'the capitalist road,' 'bourgeois remnants,' and 'modern revisionism.' Without trying to describe each of these in detail, one may say that the image of modern revisionism is the one that has been recently expressed with greatest intensity and perhaps greatest fear. For modern revisionism represents both an external danger, as embodied by the visible friend-turned-enemy, the Soviet Union, and an internal one of an insidious personal nature. It is a form of degeneracy, of inner death, experienced by those who once knew the true path to revolutionary immortality but, through a combination of moral weakness or shadowy conspiracy, strayed from it. Much more than the other negative images, modern revisionism also looms closer to an immediate possibility.

But why now? Why the crisis in boundaries—in revolutionary immortality—at this time? There is much evidence that the Cultural Revolution represents the culmination of a series of conflicts surrounding totalistic visions and national campaigns, of an increasing inability to fulfill the visions or achieve the transformations of the physical and spiritual environment claimed by the campaigns. And these conflicts went on all through the late 1950s and early 1960s, and found dramatic expression in what was surely the most remarkable campaign of all prior to the Cultural Revolution, that of the Great Leap Forward of 1958.

The 'Great Leap,' in brief, was a heroic attempt to achieve rapid industrialization and collectivization by making extensive use of the bare hands and the pure minds of the Chinese people. It was really an attempt to break through ordinary boundaries of revolutionary accomplishment, and to outdo revolutionary rivals in the rapid march toward a state of communism. Such visions of transformation had become very basic to Chinese Communist (and more specifically Maoist) practice—and in many cases had been so brilliantly realized—that they could not be abandoned without a sense that the fundamental momentum of the revolution, its life force, was ebbing. But whether one attributed the Great Leap's failure (and, despite some accomplishments, it was essentially a failure) to insufficient revolutionary zeal, as Mao clearly did, or to an excess of the same, as did Liu Shao-chi and other so-called pragmatists, all came to feel anxious about the life of the revolution.

Moreover, the regime's subsequent economic backtracking and cultural liberalization (during the year 1961 to 1962), which was apparently implemented by the pragmatists, despite Mao's resistance, also contributed to these conflicts. That is, measures deemed necessary for national recovery encouraged precisely the kinds of personal freedom and self-interest readily viewed later on, within Chinese Communist ideology, as "decadent" forms of "individualism" and "economism"—as forms of "degeneracy" and "decay"—as death-tainted threats to the immortal revolutionary vision.

The Chinese have also had to cope with a more concrete form of death anxiety, as stimulated by America's aggressive policy in Vietnam, and by the fear of war with America. It is very difficult to evaluate how great a part the fear of war with America has played in the Cultural Revolution. Generally speaking, the Cultural Revolution seems to stem from within Chinese Communist revolutionary practice, but its shape could well have been influenced by this fear. What one can say is that the Cultural Revolution itself appears to be more a quest for a collective sense of revolutionary power than an actual mobilization of military power to combat an outside enemy.

The activist response to symbolic death, or to what might be called unmastered death anxiety, is a quest for rebirth. One could in fact view the entire Cultural Revolution as a demand for the renewal of Communist life. It is, in other words, a call for reassertion of revolutionary immortality. Now, in Maoist China, this has meant nothing less than an all-consuming experience of death and rebirth, an induced catastrophe, together with a prescription for reconstituting the world being destroyed.

The agents of this attempted rebirth are of great importance: I refer to those called upon to extend revolutionary boundaries, the Red Guards. The tenderness of their years —they included not only youths in their early twenties or late teens, but children of thirteen and fourteen—has been striking to everyone, and then much too quickly attributed to political necessity alone. The assumption here is that, having alienated most of the more mature population by his extreme policies, Mao had no choice but to call upon the young. But I believe one must look beyond such explanations (whatever their partial truth) to the wider symbolism of the Red Guard movement.

The Red Guards first began to appear during the early summer of 1966. Without going into detail about their emergence, one can say that they were called forth by the Maoists and continuously manipulated from above, but that there were also elements of spontaneity, as there inevitably are in such movements, especially in youth movements. Only after an official public confirmation and blessing from Mao Tse-tung, during a gigantic dawn rally on August 18th of that year, did the Red Guard really take on national, and even international, significance. Within a few days after that, tens of thousands of youngsters, with identifying red armbands, were roaming throughout Peking, and before long, throughout the entire country.

From the beginning, the battle cry of the Red Guard was the triumph of youth over age, of the new over the old. Hence the Red Guard's announced early goal of totally destroying the "four olds": old ideas, old culture, old customs, and old habits. The human targets selected by the young militants for mental and physical abuse were referred to as "old fogies of the landlord and bourgeois class," as "the revisionist clique of old men," and a bit later, as "old men in authority" and "old gentlemen who follow the capitalist road." The Red Guards themselves were heralded as "young people who had declared war on the old world." But in their attack upon old age and decay, they were, psychologically speaking, declaring war upon death itself.

Great stress was also placed on their 'purity,' and at the beginning only those who had certain kinds of class and family backgrounds were permitted to become Red Guards. Their targets, in contrast, were associated with ultimate impurity, as designated members of the "five black" categories: landlords, rich peasants, counter-revolutionaries, "bad elements," and rightists. One observer of the official Chinese film taken of that August 18th rally—noting the extraordinary dawn scene of a million people gathered in the great square, singing "The East is Red," Mao Tse-tung powerful in his presence though walking slowly and stiffly, then moving out among the masses on the arm of a teen-age girl—spoke of the formation of a "new community." I would suggest that this new community, in a symbolic sense, is a community of immortals, of men, women and children entering into a new relationship with the eternal revolutionary process. An event of this kind is meant to convey a blending of the immortal cultural and racial substance of the Chinese as a people with the equally immortal Communist revolution.

On other occasions as well, the Red Guard created an image of young people touched by grace, bestowing their anointed state on everyone around them. But they have also had a different face. Theirs has been the task of inducing the catastrophe, of, in their own words, "breaking and smashing," of initiating widespread agitation and disruption while spreading the message that this was what the country required. They became a strange young band of wandering zealots in search of evil and impurity, in their own terms "anti-bureaucratic" and "anti-authority."

The objects of Red Guard activism varied enormously. There was the invasion of homes of people in the "five black" categories, with confiscation of belongings. There were various forms of physical and verbal abuse, including the ritual of parading certain people through the streets in dunce caps; attacks upon temples and churches; destruction of art objects; destruction of certain forms of clothing, and of foreign made objects of various kinds, including dolls and playing cards; and the replacement of certain forms of burial ceremonies with simple cremation. And then there were the somewhat ludicrous dimensions of such things as the demand that traffic signals be reversed, that the red have the properly positive connotation of "go," or that military drill be changed from "eyes right" to "eyes left" and so on, even to the point of renaming Peking "East Is Red." But the Red Guard embodied a consistent principle, and that was the principle of renewal—an image of perpetual youth, really perpetual life, that was both revolutionary and Chinese.

In struggling to extend the boundaries of revolution in ways that I have been describing, there was a continuous interplay of what I would call purity and power. Without describing this at great length, I want to suggest that purity and power were inseparable, and indeed always are inseparable in such movements. There has been a general tendency on the part of many outside observers to claim that an image of purity has been no more than a decoy and a mask for the hunger for power lurking beneath. But the assumption can be highly misleading. Rather than constituting antagonistic motivations, purity and power are in fact psychologically inseparable as well.

Two features of the Cultural Revolution epitomize this purity-power constellation. The first is the (at least temporary) use of the Paris Commune of 1871 as a model, and the second (perhaps much more important), the dual role of the Army. Looking only at the second for a moment, one must point out that on the one hand, the Army has been the model for purity. It is the Army that really owns most of the heroic image of the Long March, and the Army served as a general model for much of the Cultural Revolution, including the supplying of dramatic examples of military men as martyrs. On the other hand, the power that the Army represented was necessary to call into play in order to pursue the Cultural Revolution and implement it. For both purity and power are ultimately associated with some kind of divine, or at least more than human image, 'godlike' and 'god-given,' whether in the sense of virtue so absolute as to transcend moral frailty, or of an immortal legacy—the Mandate of Heaven or Divine Right of Kings—justifying control over other men. To put it another way, power becomes the harnessing of purity for an immortal quest.

What about the extraordinary entity known as the Thought of Mao Tse-tung? Here we come to the phenomenon of immortalization of words. But how is this entity, or body of thought, related to the extension of revolutionary boundaries we have been discussing? We may first say that the man and his words have fused into a powerful image which became the essence of revolutionary immortality as well as the energizer for its quest. This is, of course, by no means the first time that a political leader has been made into a divinity, but few in the past could have matched Mao in the superlatives used, the number of celebrants, or the thoroughness with which the message of glory has been disseminated.

All cultures, of course, have ways of rendering the word sacred, and none more than China. Relevant here is the Confucian focus upon the name as a means of ordering all of human life, and also the traditional principle of "rectification of names," which required not only that each live according to the rules governing his category of existence ("Let the ruler be ruler, the minister be minister; let the father be father and the son, son"), but that where disparity existed, the *man* undergo whatever moral change was required for him to fit the name.

One must also consider Mao's own way with words. He has been by no means merely the bearer of venerable tendencies, but has over the years made use of a word-centered tradition in the special fashion of a great contemporary leader.

If we examine more closely Mao's thought, the usual commentary about it has stressed (perhaps rightly) its preoccupation with principles of "struggle" and "contradictions" and of "rectification" and reform. But what I think has not been adequately recognized is a special quality of tone and content that, more than any other, shaped the psychic contours of the Cultural Revolution. I refer here to a kind of *existential absolute, an insistence upon all-or-none confrontation with death*. Mao always further insists that the confrontation be rendered meaningful, that it be associated with a mode of transcendence. One must risk all, not only because one has little to lose but because even in death one has much to gain.

This quality of thought is amply illustrated by many selections contained in the little red bible of the Cultural Revolution, *Quotations from Chairman Mao Tse-tung*. One important chapter takes its title from Mao's 1944 essay, "Serve the People," and includes two comments about death and dying taken from the earlier essay. The first presents a simple definition of a "worthy death": "Wherever there is struggle there is sacrifice, and death is a common occurrence. But we have the interests of the people and the sufferings of the great majority at heart, and when we die for the people it is a worthy death." The cautionary sentence that follows—"Nevertheless, we should do our best to avoid unnecessary sacrifices"—does not alter the message. The second and more probing passage makes use of a classical image: "All men must die, but death can vary in its significance. The ancient Chinese writer Szuma Chien said, 'Though death befalls all men alike, it may be heavier than Mount Tai or lighter than a feather.' To die for the people is heavier than Mount Tai, but to work for the fascists and die for the exploiters and oppressors is lighter than a feather." Here "weight" is equated with lasting significance: a death becomes "heavier than Mount Tai" because it contributes to the immortal revolutionary process of the Chinese people. Mao encourages everyone to cultivate such a death and thereby, during life, enhance his individual *sense* of immortality.

One could also point to Mao's famous "paper tiger" image which has been applied to imperialism, to all reactionaries, to America and, as everybody knows, to nuclear weapons. What Mao keeps telling his people, in a great variety of ways, is that, above all, one need not fear death at the hands of the enemy. He speaks in a tone of transcendence, and conveys to the revolutionary a message which seems to say: Death does not really exist for you; there is nothing to fear. Mao put forth this message very vividly as early as 1919 during the cultural revolution of that year, the epochal May Fourth Movement: "What is the greatest force? The greatest force is that of the union of the popular masses. What should we fear? We should not fear heaven. We should not fear ghosts. We should not fear the dead. We should not fear the bureaucrats. We should not fear the militarists. We should not fear the capitalists."

A leader who can instill these transcendent principles in his followers can turn the most extreme threat of disintegration into an ordered certainty of mission, convert the most incapacitating death anxiety into a death-conquering calm of near invincibility. He can, in fact, become the omnipotent guide sought by all totalist movements—precisely the meaning of the characterization of Mao during the Cultural Revolution as the "Great Leader, Great Teacher, Great Supreme Commander and Great Helmsman." The Thought of Mao becomes not so much a precise theory of society as, in the traditional Chinese sense, a Way, a call to a particular mode of being on behalf of a transcendent purpose.

Behind this Way are two psychological assumptions long prominent in Mao's thought but never so overtly insisted upon as during the Cultural Revolution. The first is an image of the human mind as infinitely malleable, capable of being reformed, transformed, and rectified without limit. The second is a related vision of the will as all-powerful, even to the extent that (in his own words) "the subjective creates the objective." These two assumptions raise problems about boundaries which we shall soon discuss in relationship to the concept of 'psychism.' What can be said here is that Mao the man and the Thought of Mao Tse-tung converge into an immortalizing corpus.

The epitome of this immortalizing process is reached in another passage which conveys the aura of worship which came to characterize the Cultural Revolution: "The thought of Mao Tse-tung is the sun in our heart, is the root of our life, is the source of all our strength. Through this, man becomes unselfish, daring, intelligent, able to do everything; he is not conquered by any difficulty and can conquer every enemy. The thought of Mao Tse-tung transforms man's ideology, transforms the Fatherland . . . through this the oppressed people of the world will rise."

The Maoist corpus is elevated to an all-consuming prophecy: it nurtures men, predicts their future, and changes the world to accomplish its own prediction; it sets in motion spiritual forces against which nothing can stand. It can, in other words, break down all boundaries which might restrict the revolution, and thereby render immortal the revolutionary community.

Now, this verbal genuflection before Mao has undoubtedly at times taken on the quality of tired ritual—of cliché for all occasions. But I want to stress that the embrace of the immortal corpus can indeed inspire unusual effort and accomplishment. I think we have to assume various combinations of ritualistic cliché and authenticity in widely disseminated claims of the marvelous contributions of Mao's Thought to such large tasks as the drilling of oil wells, the construction of great modern airports, and the completion in record time of highly advanced and elaborate equipment for the steel industry. And when we are told how villagers, in true Maoist fashion, have "transformed heaven and earth" in achieving enormous victories over wind, sand, flood, and drought, there is no reason for us to doubt that some of the people involved in these projects felt energized by the Maoist phrases being chanted—any more than we would doubt that many who did not said that they did. (Concerning the claim that Mao's Thought was responsible for the unexpectedly early completion and successful testing of a hydrogen bomb [in June 1967], we have reason to believe that the major contribution of Maoism was to leave the nuclear scientists alone.) Certainly men and women in a variety of situations—and not only Chinese—have felt themselves strengthened by allying themselves to this immortal corpus.

One might have been tempted to dismiss the entire cult of Mao and his Thought as no more than sycophantic indulgence of an old man's vanity, were it not for the life that Mao has lived, and the impact he has made upon the Chinese people. He has in fact, and this is of the utmost importance, virtually lived out precisely the existential absolute he has advocated. No twentieth-century life has come closer than his to the great myth of the hero—with its 'road of trials' or prolonged death encounter, and its mastery of that encounter in a way that enhances the life of one's people. It is this conquest of death that I see as the central theme of the myth of the hero, rather than that of the Oedipus complex, as claimed in the classical Freudian literature. Mao has throughout his life had unusual sensitivity to death imagery, and to survivor guilt in particular. But rather than being incapacitated by such feelings he has, in the manner of all great leaders, applied them to the larger historical crises of his day.

Mao's relationship to the myth of the hero is also enhanced by certain characteristics of his personal and revolutionary style that reveal a man closely attuned to the pulse of immortality. These include his celebrated 'revolutionary romanticism' (a designation which would sound highly derogatory to most communist ears but which official Chinese commentaries have associated with revolutionary courage and imagination), his affinity for guerrilla warfare and his brilliant achievements in that kind of warfare, his so-called 'heaven-storming' approach to the transformation of Chinese society, his special affinity for outlaws as well as for the common people—and in addition, his standing as a poet, and the great stress in his poetry upon various forms of transcendence and upon ways in which fallen revolutionary comrades have been immortalized.

Rather than speak of Mao as a father figure or mother figure for his countrymen, we do better to see him as a *death-conquering hero who became the embodiment of Chinese immortality*.

But over the course of Mao's later career, we may say that word not only becomes flesh, but it becomes *his* flesh. The man-word corpus is increasingly represented as *absolutely* identical with China's destiny. And we sense ourselves witnesses to the tragic transition from the great leader to the despot.

A crucial factor in this transition has been Mao's struggle with technology, and his resort to what I have called psychism. By this ungainly term I mean to suggest a confusion between inner and outer worlds, in Mao's case an exaggerated stress upon revolutionary will in the attempt to achieve technological goals. At issue here are the boundaries (in the sense of inner distinctions man must make) between self and things, between mind and its material products.

In evaluating Mao's dilemmas, one must keep in mind that man has been struggling with these boundaries since he fashioned his first tool, and that there presently exists a world-wide rebellion against the overwhelming influence of twentieth-century 'things,' and against the increasing psychic tendency for man to re-create himself according to a technological model. In this sense China's struggles with technology are part of a vast confusion that envelops the entire planet.

But her struggles are intensified by her relatively backward position within a series of keenly felt rivalries—with the more 'developed' countries, with the white West, and with the Soviet Union. There is a strong Chinese feeling that technology can be a route to the recovery of past cultural glory. Hence, Mao's hunger for technology, together with his insistence that it be acquired on his own spiritual terms, can be seen as the latest episode in China's hundred-year struggle to cope with the modern world according to the unworkable principle of grafting alien Western knowledge and technique onto an immutably Chinese 'essence.'

We are not surprised that psychism of various kinds emerged very strongly during the movement epitomizing Mao's confrontation with technology, that of the Great Leap Forward. And the kind of confrontation and difficulty the Chinese encountered in that movement was epitomized by the well-publicized images of backyard furnaces for the smelting of pig iron: at first a source of wonder as they appeared where no furnace had ever been, heralding exciting innovations in production by the people, but then (as one observer put it) "dissolv[ing] into piles of mud and brick after a few rains."

Now the Great Leap was by no means a complete failure. Some production increased, useful small industries were developed, and various forms of revolutionary practice were promoted. But on the whole, the country was left in profound economic disorder, a large percentage of its plants and factories functioning erratically, without statistical control or standardization, and in many cases having to be abandoned entirely.

What becomes clear in examining the entire tone of the Great Leap is *the extent to which the passions behind the vision of immortal Chinese revolutionary and cultural substance took precedence over accurate perception of the environment and of the requirements for altering it.* In brief, many of the requirements for technology were simply ignored. And here we are dealing with what I call a psychistic fallacy, an assumption of the interchangeability of psychic state and technology. Technology is sought, but feelings are cultivated. The psychological and socioeconomic reverberations of the Great Leap are undoubtedly still being felt in China, and one might view the Cultural Revolution itself as a kind of 'Second Leap' in response to a Maoist need to vindicate the first one.

Psychism, then, in the confrontation with technology, set an important boundary to the revolutionary aspirations of this great movement. But there have been other boundaries and impediments as well.

In my earlier study of Chinese thought reform (or "brainwashing") I suggested three such limitations, which I believe also apply in the Cultural Revolution: mounting inner antagonisms or the "hostility of suffocation"; the effective penetration of "idea-tight milieu control" by outside influences that undermine the closed communication system; and a "law of diminishing conversions" operating among those subjected to repeated reform experiences, according to which inner enthusiasm is increasingly replaced by outward compliance.

One finds extensive evidence of the hostility of suffocation, not only in observations of visitors and defectors, but in the tones of anger and hatred from all sides in the public and semi-public exchanges of accusations and counteraccusations throughout the Cultural Revolution—tones startling even to those familiar with the explosive series of mass campaigns carried out by the Communist regime in the past. Initially one may say that the anger and hatred were themselves part of a command performance, but over the course of the Cultural Revolution they tended to become more unfocused and antithetical to the purposes of the movement. Another manifestation of the hostility of suffocation went beyond hostility itself, and took the form of withdrawal from the overall psychic and physical struggle. Reports appeared of groups of alienated Chinese youth known as "wanderers," characterized by their disinterest in political matters and their desire to pursue their own small pleasures.

Concerning the second psychological limitation, the undermining of milieu control by ideas from the outside, we may again point to the specter of modern revisionism. For it seems clear that Chinese minds have been indelibly marked by revisionist images—especially by those stressing liberalization and pragmatism as alternatives to totalism and psychism. Concrete evidence of this has been the appearance in China of a 'New Trend,' apparently influenced by revisionist as well as by independent Marxist principles, and possibly by egalitarian non-Marxist ones as well. Human history can be defined as the continuous spread of ideas and images from mind to mind and group to group, and in our present electronic age it becomes particularly futile to attempt to seal off any collectivity from impinging outside currents.

The third limitation on psychism and totalism, the 'law of diminishing conversions,' follows directly upon the other two. Here we encounter the built-in contradiction of psychism: in its zeal to replace technology with mind, it tends to interfere with precisely the internal work necessary to accomplish real individual conversion and general social transformation. While extolling the mind and the will as creators of external reality, the Cultural Revolution has lacked the patient assurance and steady effort necessary for genuine reshaping (or realignment) of mental processes. This assurance and effort could be said to have been present during earlier thought reform campaigns, though even then results tended to be mixed. The Cultural Revolution utilized such standard thought-reform elements as criticism and self-criticism, group-mediated shame and guilt, and the by now classic Maoist subject matter. But public demonstration was substituted for internal experience, activism for psychic work, violence for persuasion—and ultimately, one suspects, uneasy obedience for significant inner change.

Confronted by these psychological limitations, Mao begins to manifest what has been called the "end of charisma" —the loss of some of the magnetic hold he has had upon his followers. His mode of immortality falling into question, he becomes the target of ambivalence and hostility previously muted and transcended by identification with his greatness.

A fundamental boundary here has to do with that elusive but still important concept of 'human nature'—a concept which has been emphasized by Russian and Eastern European revisionism as part of a reassertion of the importance of the individual, and vehemently denounced during the Cultural Revolution. I do not mean human nature as a rigidly set entity but as a general psychobiological potential within a particular (though always changing) cultural and historical matrix. Human nature thus understood is highly flexible, yet at the same time an imposer of limits. One of these limits is the need for a certain amount of harmony between the evidence of the senses and socially shared images of self and world.

All I have been saying suggests that psychism and the quest for totality are limited by the nature of the mind, the body, and the world. While all three are aspects of a metaphysical whole, they cannot be substituted for one another, not even in the name of a transcendent revolutionary vision.

In many significant ways the Cultural Revolution may be viewed as a Last Stand. It has been, as we have seen, the last stand of a great revolutionary against internal and external forces pressing him along that treacherous path from hero to despot. Similarly it has been the last stand of a collective expression of early revolutionary glory which he epitomized. And it is perceived on several symbolic levels as a last stand against death itself—of the leader, the revolution, and individual man in general.

But it also can be a last stand of another less recognized entity, one that I would call 'militant rectitude'—a state of politicized straight-and-narrow moral earnestness pursued with unrelenting passion. Militant rectitude is an existential style that seems oddly old-fashioned during the latter part of our diffusely absurd twentieth century. Containing Confucian and Christian as well as communist contributions, it was epitomized during the Cultural Revolution by the totally mobilized, self-negating Red Guard, unswervingly dedicated to living out the immortalizing vision. What threatens militant rectitude is a very different kind of temporary being I have already described as Protean man. We know him to stand in direct contrast to militant rectitude—in his psychological style of interminable exploration and flux, and in his capacity for relatively easy shifts in belief and identification. He is the antithesis of militant rectitude in another aspect as well: his profound inner sense of absurdity has been given prominent expression in a prevailing tone of mockery.

I have suggested that Protean man seems to be emerging everywhere, including East Asia, as an important psychological type. I in fact encountered Protean patterns in refugee intellectuals from the Chinese mainland, most of them young, whom I interviewed in depth in 1954 and in 1955, suggesting that it has been at least latent in China for some time, even if covered over by Maoist images of purity and rectitude. Nor is this surprising, since the Protean style emerges from a radical breakdown in man's most structured relationship to traditional symbols—from psychohistorical dislocation—which China has over recent decades experienced in the extreme. Does all this suggest the likelihood of a pragmatic turn in China? I think one has to be cautious about drawing short-term political conclusions from general psychological observations, but I think that one can also say that such a turn would be consistent with the technological and psychological limitations to Maoist psychism we have discussed, as well as with the evolution of Protean man. The fact is that the turn toward pragmatism has already begun. A program of pragmatic retreat is described in the language of victory; a pause (or halt) in the extreme pursuit of revolutionary immortality is represented as its attainment. All is done, and long after Mao's death will continue to be done, in the leader's name (though diminished, his charisma surely remains strong enough to be, in Weber's term, 'ritualized,' and one must also keep in mind Mao's own pragmatic side).

Of great importance for the future is the degree to which a post-Cultural Revolution regime can (in the psychological idiom I have been using) hold out to the Chinese people a form of symbolic immortality less extreme and less dependent upon psychism than that recently put forth. We would expect a vision of revolutionary immortality to remain important, but possibly in more open combination with new forms and other modes—biological, creative, theological, natural, and experiential. In the meantime, we may expect that the Cultural Revolution will leave its traumatic impact in more ways than can now be imagined. Yet I believe it would be very rash to assume that a regime that has so recently commanded so much psychic power would suddenly cease to possess any at all. Not only does the Chinese Communist regime remain viable, but so does the overall phenomenon of 'Chinese Communist culture.'

It is in the nature of great men and great revolutions to be dissatisfied with their accomplishments, however extraordinary, and to set themselves the task of eliminating boundaries that will not give way. If this be the meaning of tragedy, the tragedy is not merely theirs. Nor is the present task of recovering from Mao's excesses—and evolving an equilibrium between life and death appropriate to our age—that of China alone. We have in fact been witnessing very different approaches to revolution, cultural and otherwise, elsewhere, approaches equally concerned with questions of limits and boundaries.

THE NEW HISTORY

There are psychological and historical stirrings of a revolutionary nature throughout the world, especially (but by no means exclusively) among the young. They are influenced by, but at the same time independent of, the Maoist visions described in the last chapter. Indeed they can be understood as part of a vast effort to bring about what we may term a New History.

What is a New History? And why do the young seek one? Let me define a New History as a radical and widely shared re-creation of the forms of human culture—biological, experiential, institutional, technological, aesthetic, and interpretative. The newness of these cultural forms derives not from their spontaneous generation but from extension and transformations of existing psychic and physical components, that is, from previously unknown or inadequately known combinations. A New History, then, is both an extension and a resetting of boundaries.

The shapers of a New History can be political revolutionaries, revolutionary thinkers, extreme holocausts, or technological breakthroughs. These and the great events surrounding them, in different ways, cause, reflect, and symbolize historical shifts. I suggested earlier that the combination of Nazi genocide and the American atomic bombings of Hiroshima and Nagasaki terminated man's sense of limits concerning his self-destructive potential, and thereby inaugurated an era in which he is devoid of assurance of living on eternally as a species. It has taken almost twenty-five years for beginning formulations of the significance of these events to emerge—formulations which cannot be separated from the technological developments of the same quarter century, or from the increasing sense of the universal world-society that has accompanied them.

Our own New History, then, is built upon the ultimate paradox of two competing and closely related images: that of technologically induced historical extinction, and that of man's increasingly profound awareness of himself as a single species. It may be more correct to say that this is just one image, extraordinarily divided.

I think we should take seriously the assertion by the young framers of the celebrated 1962 Port Huron Statement of the Students for a Democratic Society, still something of a manifesto for the American New Left, that: "Our work is guided by the sense that we may be the last generation in the experiment with living." What I wish to stress is the overriding significance for every post-Hiroshima generation of precisely this threat of historical extinction. The end of the next era becomes associated, psychologically speaking, with the end of everything. And even those who deny any special concern with this threat share in the general undercurrent of death anxiety.

This anxiety becomes closely associated with other symbolic impairments of our time, with the confusions of the knowledge revolution and the unprecedented dissemination of half-knowledge through media whose psychological impact has barely begun to be discerned.

There is a very real sense in which the world itself has become a 'total environment,' a closed psychic chamber with continuous reverberations bouncing about chaotically and dangerously. The symbolic death perceived, then, is this combination of formlessness and totality, of the inadequacy of existing forms and imprisonment within them. The boundaries of the environment are felt to be in one sense absolute, in another nonexistent. And the young are exquisitely sensitive to this kind of 'historical death,' whatever their capacity for resisting an awareness of the biological kind. They are struck by the fact that most of mankind simply goes about its business, as if these extreme dislocations did not exist—as if there were no such thing as ultimate technological violence or existence rendered absurd. The war in Vietnam did not create these murderous incongruities, but it does exemplify them, and it consumes American youth in them. No wonder, then, that, in their symbolic questions, or (to use Cassirer's phrase), in their "conversations with themselves," the young everywhere ask: "How can we bring the world—and ourselves—back to life?"

Students of revolution and rebellion have recognized the close relationship of both to death symbolism, and to visions of transcending death by achieving an eternal historical imprint. Hannah Arendt speaks of revolution as containing an "all-pervasive preoccupation with permanence, with a 'perpetual state . . . for . . . posterity.'" And Albert Camus describes insurrection, "in its exalted and tragic forms," as "a prolonged protest against death, a violent accusation against the universal death penalty," and as "the desire for immortality." But Camus also stresses the rebel's "appeal to the essence of being," his quest "not . . . for life, but for reasons for living." And this brings us to an all-important question concerning mental participation in revolution: what is the place of ideology, and of images and ideas, and of the self in relationship to all three?

Most of the revolutionary ideologies of the past have been notable in providing elaborate blueprints for individual and collective immortality, specifications of ultimate cause and ultimate effect, theological in tone and scientific in claim. For present-day revolutionaries to reject these Cartesian litanies is to take seriously some of the important psychological and historical insights of the last few decades. For they are rejecting an oppressive ideological totalism—with its demand for control of all communication in a milieu, its imposed guilt and cult of purity and confession, its loading of the language, its principles of doctrine over person and even of the dispensing of existence itself (in the sense that sharp lines are drawn between those whose right to exist can be recognized and those who possess no such right). This rejection, at its best, represents a quest by the young for a new kind of revolution—one perhaps no less enduring in historical impact, but devoid of the claim to omniscience, and of the catastrophic chain of human manipulations stemming from that claim. In other words, the young resist the suffocating personal boundaries imposed by earlier revolutions.

It is of course possible that their anti-ideological stance could turn out to be a transitory phenomenon, a version of the euphoric denial of dogma that so frequently appears during the early moments of revolution, only to be overwhelmed by absolutist doctrine and suffocating organization in the name of revolutionary discipline. Yet there is reason for believing that the present antipathy to total ideology is something more, that it is an expression of a powerful and highly appropriate contemporary style. The shift we are witnessing from fixed and total forms of ideology to more fluid *ideological fragments* represents, to a considerable degree, the emergence of contemporary or Protean man as rebel. It is an effort to remain open, while in rebellion, to the extraordinarily rich, confusing, liberating, and threatening array of contemporary historical possibilities—and to retain, in the process, a continuing capacity for shape-shifting.

The fluidity of the Protean style greatly enhances tactical leverage. For instance, Daniel Cohn-Bendit, the leader of the French student uprisings of May 1968, in an interesting dialogue with Jean-Paul Sartre, insisted that the classical Marxist-Leninist principle of the omniscient revolutionary vanguard (the working class as represented by the Communist Party) be replaced with "a much simpler and more honourable one, the theory of an active minority, acting you might say as a permanent ferment, pushing forward without trying to control events." He went on to characterize this process as "uncontrollable spontaneity." In the same spirit are the warnings of Tom Hayden, a key figure in the American New Left, to his SDS colleagues and followers, against what he calls "fixed leaders," and his insistence upon "participatory democracy" as well as upon ideology of a kind that is secondary to, and largely achieved through, revolutionary action. So widespread has this approach been that the American New Left has been characterized as more a process than a program.

I would suggest that the general principle of "uncontrollable spontaneity" represents a meeting ground between tactic and deeper psychological inclination. The underlying inclination consists precisely of the Protean style of multiple identifications, shifting beliefs, and constant search for new combinations that extend both individual-psychological and political boundaries. Whatever its pitfalls, this style of revolutionary behavior is an attempt to mobilize twentieth-century fluidity as a weapon against two kinds of stagnation: the old, unresponsive institutions (universities, governments, families), and the newly-emerging but fixed technological visions (people 'programmed' by computers in a 'technotronic society'). The young thus feel hemmed in by boundaries formed both by legacies of the past and visions of the future.

Throughout the world, the young seek active involvement in the institutional decisions governing their lives, new paths of significance as alternatives to consuming and being consumed, and liberating rhythms of individual and (especially) community existence. Nonspecific and ephemeral as these goals may seem, they are early expressions of a quest for historical rebirth, for re-attachment to the Great Chain of Being, for reassertion of a viable sense of immortality.

The French example is again revealing in its extraordinary flowering of graffiti. Here one must take note of the prominence of the genre—of the informal slogan-on-the-wall virtually replacing formal revolutionary doctrine—no less than the content. But one is struck by the stress of many of the slogans, sometimes to the point of intentional absurdity, upon enlarging the individual life space, on saying yes to more and no to less. Characteristic were such slogans as "Think of your desires as realities," "Prohibiting is forbidden," "Imagination in power," and "Imagination is revolution." Sartre made an apt comment upon both the graffiti and the young revolutionaries themselves when he said, "I would like to describe what you have done as extending the field of possibilities."

Precisely such extending of the field of possibilities is at the heart of the world-wide youth rebellion, for hippies no less than political radicals—and at the heart of the Protean insistence upon continuous psychic re-creation of the self. Around this image of unlimited extension and perpetual re-creation, as projected into a dimly imagined future, the young seek to create a new mode of *revolutionary* immortality.

Of enormous importance for these rebellions is another basic component of the Protean style, the spirit of mockery. While young rebels are by no means immune from the most pedantic and humorless discourse, they come alive to others and themselves only when giving way to—or seizing upon —their very strong inclination toward mockery. The mocking political rebel merges with the hippie and with a variety of exponents of pop culture to 'put on'—that is, mislead or deceive by means of some form of mockery or absurdity— his uncomprehending cohorts, his elders, or anyone in authority. (Despite important differences, there has always been a fundamental unity in the rebellions of hippies and young radicals, which is perhaps just now becoming fully manifest.) In dress, hair, and general social and sexual style, the mocking rebel is not only "extending the field of possibilities," but making telling commentary—teasing, ironic, contemptuous—on the absurd folkways of 'the others.' The mockery can be gentle and even loving, or it can be bitter and provocative in the extreme.

One thinks of the widely publicized slogan of the Columbia uprising: "Up against the wall, motherfucker!" with its complex relationships to blacks and whites, to police and their antagonists, and to the principle of authority in general. The bandying about of the phrase was a way of playing with, and mocking, an image of ultimate violation and of retribution for that violation.

The tone of mockery can be a source of great unifying power. At its more affirmative border are such slogans of the French students as: "We are all undesirables!" or the much more powerful "We are all German Jews!" The slogans refer directly to the origins of Cohn-Bendit, the student leader, but their significance extends much further. They mock not only anti-Semitism and national-racial chauvinism, but the overall process of victimization itself, and the 'old history' for harboring such victimization. At this affirmative border of mockery, then, and at the far reaches of Protean style, is a call for man to cease his folly in dividing himself into pseudo-species and to respond to the ethical and technological mandate to see himself as the single species he is.

Mockery thus breaks down the false boundaries imposed by victimization, and encourages every variety of odd combination. One can observe a related if much more confusing impulse toward inclusiveness in the diversity of ideological fragments young rebels embrace. Thus hippies, for their experiments with the self, draw upon Eastern and Western mysticism, chemically induced ecstasy, and various traditions, new and old, of polymorphous sexuality. Young radicals may incorporate any of these aspects of hippie culture, and combine them with ideas and images drawn from many different revolutionary experiences (pre-Marxist utopians, anarchists, Marx, Trotsky, Lenin, Rosa Luxemburg, Mao, Castro, Guevara, Debray, Ho, Gandhi, Fanon, Malcolm X, Martin Luther King, Stokely Carmi-

chael, and H. Rap Brown); from recent psychological and
social theorists (Sartre, Camus, C. Wright Mills, Herbert
Marcuse, Norman Brown, Erik Erikson, Abraham Maslow,
and Paul Goodman); and from just about any kind of
evolving cultural style (derived from jazz or black power or
'soul,' from the small-group movement and the Esalen-type
stress upon joy, or from camp-mockery of Victorian or
other retrospectively amusing periods), including all of the
revolutionary and intellectual traditions just mentioned.

The overall process can be seen as a revolutionary equiv-
alent to the artist's inclination to borrow freely, selectively,
impressionistically, and distortingly from contemporaries as
a means of finding his own way. To dismiss all of this as a
'style revolution,' as some have, is to miss the point—unless
one is aware of the sense in which style is everything. One
does better to speak of a 'revolution of forms,' of a quest for
images of rebirth which reassert connectedness, and as a
'process revolution' consistent with the principles of action
painting and kinetic sculpture, in which active rebelling
both expresses and creates the basic images of rebellion.
The novelist Donald Barthelme's statement, "Fragments are
the only form I trust," has ramifications far beyond the literary. However severe the problems posed by such a principle for social and especially political revolutions, we deceive ourselves unless we learn to focus upon these shifting
forms—in styles of life as well as in relations to institutions
and ideas. Indeed we require a little revolutionizing of our
psychological assumptions, so that both the young and the
old can be understood, not as bound by static behavioral
categories, but as in continuous historical motion.

There has been much discussion about young rebels' selection of the university as a primary target for recent upheavals. Many distinguished commentators have cautioned students about the dangers of confusing the vulnerable centers of learning they attack, and for periods of time 'bring down,' with society at large. Stephen Spender put the matter eloquently when he said that "However much the university needs a revolution, and the society needs a revolution, it would be disastrous . . . not to keep the two revolutions apart." He went on to point out, as have others also, that the university is "an arsenal from which [student-rebels] can draw the arms from which they can change society"; and that "To say, 'I won't have a university until society has a revolution,' is as though Karl Marx were to say 'I won't go to the reading room of the British Museum until it has a revolution.' " Yet wise as these cautionary thoughts undoubtedly are, one also has to consider the ways in which the university's special symbolic significance makes it all too logical (if at times unfortunate) a target for would-be revolutionaries.

For the university is unique as a formative area. It is the place where the prevailing concepts of a society are simultaneously and with varying weightings presented, imposed, examined and criticized—where intellectual and ethical boundaries are examined and either narrowed or extended, but in any case redefined. The university is indeed a training ground for available occupational slots in society, as young rebels are quick to point out, and can, at its worst, approach a technical instrument in the hands of the military-industrial complex. But it can also be precisely the opposite, a training ground for undermining social institutions, as the young rebels themselves attest to by the extent to which they are campus products.

In most cases, the university is a great many things in between. It provides for students four years of crucial personal transition, a *rite de passage* from relatively unformed adolescence to a relatively formed adulthood. And the fact that many are likely to move through continuing Protean explorations during the post-university years renders especially important whatever initial adult formation the university makes possible. For these reasons, and because students and teachers are *there,* the university is the best place for the rebellious young to confront their ostensible mentors— their 'formative fathers'—and thereby both define themselves and make a statement about society at large. The statement they make has to do not only with social inequities and outmoded institutions but with the general historical dislocations of everyone. And in this sense the target of the young is not so much the university, or the older generation, as the continuing commitment of both to the discredited past.

Now, one can hardly speak of definitive conclusions about something just beginning. Nor would I claim a position of omniscient detachment from the events of the New History—I have in no way been immune from the complex combinations of feelings about them known to my generation of Left intellectuals. But having earlier in this talk affirmed the significance of the New History, I wish now to suggest some of its pitfalls, and then, finally, some of our present-day potentialities for avoiding these pitfalls.

From the standpoint of the young, these pitfalls are related to what is best called 'romantic totalism.' I refer here to a post-Cartesian absolutism, to a new quest for old feelings. Its controlling image, at whatever level of consciousness, is that of *replacing history with experience.*

This is, to a considerable extent, the romanticism of the 'youth movement.' I have heard a number of thoughtful European-born intellectuals tell, with some anxiety, how the tone and atmosphere now emanating from young American rebels is reminiscent of that of the German youth movement of the late Weimar Republic (and the Hitler Youth into which it was so readily converted). What they find common to both is a cult of feeling and a disdain for restraint and reason. While I would emphasize the differences between the two groups much more than any similarities, there is a current in contemporary youth movements that is more Nietzschean than Marxist-Leninist. It consists of a stress upon what I call experiential transcendence, upon the cultivation of states of feelings so intense and so absorbing that time and death cease to exist. (Drugs are of great importance here but as part of a general quest.) The pattern becomes totalistic when it begins to tamper with history to the extent of victimizing opponents in order to reinforce these feelings; and a danger signal is the absolute denial of the principle of historical continuity.

The replacement of history with experience—with totally liberated feeling—is by no means a new idea and has long found expression in classical forms of mysticism and ecstasy. But it has reappeared with considerable force in the present-day drug revolution, and in the writings of a number of articulate spokesmen, such as Norman O. Brown. This increasing stress upon experiential forms of transcendence would seem to be related to the impairment of alternative modes of symbolic immortality I have already discussed. That is, the undermining of biological, cultural, and theological modes of immortality by both the speed of historical change, and by the threat posed by nuclear and other weapons, profoundly intensifies man's anxiety about both his death and his manner of life. One response to this anxiety, and to the quest for new forms, is the unique contemporary blending of experiential transcendence—in which boundaries of the self are felt to be eliminated—with social and political revolution.

At times entire historical traditions can be condemned or negated, largely by calling into play a single judgmental criterion: What feels revolutionary is good, what does not is counter-revolutionary. A related equally romantic pitfall is that of 'generational totalism.' The problem is not so much the slogan "Don't trust anybody over thirty," as the unconscious assumption that can be behind it: that youth power knows no limits because youth equals immortality. That is, an assumption that youth and only youth has access to boundarylessness. Conversely, members of older generations can, just as totalistically, view every innovative action of the young as destructive or 'deadly.' Indeed, the larger significance and greatest potential danger of what we call the 'generation gap' reside in differing solutions to these questions of broken historical connection and impaired sense of immortality.

The recent slogan of French students, "The young make love, the old make obscene gestures" is patronizing rather than totalistic, and its mocking blend of truth and absurdity permits a chuckle all around. But when the same students refer to older critics as "people who do not exist," or when young American radicals label everyone and everything either "relevant" ("revolutionary") or "irrelevant" ("counter-revolutionary") on the basis of whether or not the person, idea, or event is consistent or inconsistent with their own point of view—then we are dealing with something more potentially malignant. We approach the totalistic tendency I referred to before as the dispensing of existence, the drawing of a sharp line between people and non-people.

A related form of image-focused totalism is the all-encompassing concept of the 'Establishment.' Taken over from British rebels, it has come to mean everything from the American (or Russian, or just about any other) political or bureaucratic leadership, to businessmen large and small, university administrators and teachers of all colorings, and including even many of the student and youth leaders who are themselves very much at odds with people in the other categories. And just as Establishment becomes a devil-image, so do other terms—such as (in different ways) 'confrontation' and 'youth'—become god-images. At issue here is the degree to which a particular image is given a transcendent status, and is then uncritically applied to the most complex situations, in a way that makes it the start and finish of any ethical judgment or conceptual analysis.

This image-focused totalism can enter into the ultimate romanticization, that of death and immortality. While the *sense* of immortality, of unending historical continuity, is central to ordinary psychological experience, romantic totalism tends to *confuse death with immortality,* and even to equate them. And behind this confusion lurks the romantic temptation to court death in the service of immortality, to view dying and in some cases even killing as the only true avenues to immortality.

The great majority of today's radical young embrace no such imagery—they are in fact intent upon exploring the furthest outreach of the life process. But they can at times be prone to a glorification of life and death stances, so that all-or-none 'revolutionary tactics' can be applied to petty disputes, hardly worthy of these cosmic images. In such situations, their sense of mockery, especially self-mockery, deserts them, and at considerable cost.

In the last chapter I spoke of the paradoxes surrounding the romantic totalism of Mao Tse-tung and his conduct of the Chinese Cultural Revolution. Mao has nonetheless had great appeal for many young rebels throughout the world, especially because of his anti-institutional impulse.

But young rebels who embrace from afar Mao's stress on "permanent revolution" may too easily overlook the consequences of his recent programs: irreparable national dissension, convoluted and meaningless forms of violence, and extreme confusion and disillusionment among Chinese youth (as well as their elders), perhaps especially among those who initially responded most enthusiastically to the call for national transformation. Nor are young rebels in the West aware of the extent to which the Maoist vision has had to be modified and in some ways abandoned in response to the deep-seated opposition it encountered throughout China.

Intrinsic to Mao's romantic totalism is the pattern I spoke of as psychism—the confusion between mind and its material products, the attempt to control the external world and achieve strongly desired technological goals by means of intrapsychic exercises and assertions of revolutionary will. Now, the radical young in more affluent societies have a different relationship to technology; rather than desperately seeking technology, they feel trapped and suffocated by it (though they live in it, use much of it easily, and also feel some of its attraction). But they too can succumb to a similar kind of confusion, which in their case takes the form of mistaking a rewarding inner sense of group solidarity with mastery of the larger human and technological world 'outside.' The recent Maoist experience I spoke of can find its counterpart in a sequence of experiences of young rebels in the West: deep inner satisfaction accompanying bold collective action, disillusionment at the limited effects achieved, and more reckless and ineffective action with even greater group solidarity. This is not to say that all or most behavior of young rebels falls into this category—to the contrary, their political confrontations have achieved a number of striking successes largely because they were *not* merely assertions of will but could also mobilize a wide radius of opposition to outmoded and destructive academic and national policies. Yet the enormous impact of high technology in the post-modern world, and the universal tendency to surround it with vast impersonal organizations, present an ever increasing temptation to transcend the whole system (or 'bag') by means of romantic worship of the will as such, and especially the revolutionary will.

For many young rebels, Mao and Maoism are perceived less as demarcated historical person and program than as a constellation of heroic, and above all anti-bureaucratic, revolutionary images. The problem for these young rebels is to recover the historical Mao in all of his complexity—which means understanding his tragic transition from great revolutionary leader to despot. To come to terms with their own Maoism they must sort out the various elements of the original—on the one hand its call for continuous militant action on behalf of the deprived and its opposition to stagnant institutions, exhilarating principles which are consistent with evolving forms of the New History; on the other, its apocalyptic totalism, psychism, and desperate rear-guard assault upon the openness—upon the expanding psychological boundaries—of contemporary man.

Yet precisely their Protean capacities may help the young to avoid definitive commitments to these self-defeating patterns. They need not be bound by the excesses of either Cartesian rationalism or the contemporary cult of experience which feeds romantic totalism. Today's young have available for their formulations of self and world the great twentieth-century insights which liberate men from the senseless exclusions of the experiential-versus-rational bind. These insights can expand the boundaries of man's thought and his feelings in their varied combinations. I refer to the principles of symbolic thought, as expressed in the work of such people as Cassirer and Langer, and of Freud and Erikson. Of course, one can never know the exact effect of great insights upon the historical process, but it is quite possible that, with the decline of the total ideologies of the old history, ideas as such will become more important than ever in the shaping of the new. Having available an unprecedented variety of ideas and images, the young are likely to attempt more than did previous generations and perhaps make more mistakes, but also to show greater capacity to extricate themselves from a particular course and revise tactics, be-liefs, and styles—all in the service of contributing to embry-onic social forms.

What about the 'older generation,' those middle-aged Left intellectuals I referred to before? For them (us), the problem is a little different. It entails a struggle to retain (or achieve) Protean openness to the possibilities latent in the New History and to respond to that noble slogan of the French students, "Imagination in power." But at the same time, this generation does well to be its age, to call upon the experience specific to the lives of those who comprise it. It must tread the tenuous path of neither feeding upon its formative sons nor rejecting their capacity for innovative historical imagination. This is much more difficult than it may seem, because it requires those now in their forties and fifties to come to terms with the extremely painful history they have known, neither to deny that history nor to be blindly bound by it. Yet, however they may feel shunted aside by the young, there is special need for their own more seasoned, if now historically vulnerable, imaginations.

For both the intellectual young and old—together with society at large—are threatened by a violent, counter-reaction to the New History, by a restorationist impulse often centered in the lower middle classes, but not confined to any class or country. This impulse includes an urge to eliminate troublesome young rebels, along with their liberal-radical 'fathers,' and to return to a mythical past in which all was harmonious and no such disturbance of the historical peace existed. What is too often forgotten by the educated of all ages, preoccupied as they are with their own dislocations, is the extent to which such dislocations in others produce the very opposite kind of ideological inclination —in this case, a compensatory, strongly anti-Protean embrace of the simple 'purities' and absolutized boundaries of 'law and order,' rampant militarism, narrow nationalism, and personal rectitude.

If man is successful in creating the New History he must create if he is to have any history at all, then the formative fathers and sons I have spoken of must pool their resources and succeed together. Should this not happen, the failure too will be shared, whether in the form of stagnation and suffering or of shared annihilation. Like most other things in our world, the issue remains open. There is nothing absolute or inevitable about the New History and its challenge to life boundaries, except perhaps the need to bring it into being.

ROBERT JAY LIFTON holds the Foundation's Fund for Research in Psychiatry professorship at Yale University. He has been particularly concerned with the relationship between individual psychology and historical change—in China, Japan, and the United States—and with the problems surrounding the extreme historical situations of our era. He has spent almost seven years in the Far East, including an extensive stay from 1960 to 1962, during which he carried out a study of psychological patterns of Japanese youth as well as an investigation of the psychological effects of the atomic bomb in Hiroshima. He has played a prominent part in the creation of a new "psychohistorical" perspective.

Dr. Lifton was born in New York City in 1926. He taught and did research at Harvard from 1956 to 1961, where he was associated with the Center for East Asian Studies as well as the Department of Psychiatry. He lives in Woodbridge, Connecticut, with his wife, a writer, and their two small children.

He is the author of *History and Human Survival*; *Death in Life: Survivors of Hiroshima* (for which he received the National Book Award in Science in April of 1969); *Revolutionary Immortality: Mao Tse-Tung and the Chinese Cultural Revolution*; *Thought Reform and the Psychology of Totalism: A Study of "Brainwashing" in China*; and is the editor of *The Woman in America*. In addition, his writings have appeared in *Partisan Review*, *Atlantic Monthly*, *American Scholar*, the *New Republic*, and *Daedalus*, as well as various East Asian, psychiatric, and psychological journals.